Cash and credit transactions
Units 1 & 2

AAT

Central Assessment Pack

Foundation

NVQ Level 2

39849

Published November 1994 by Financial Training, 136–142 Bramley Road, London W10 6SR

Copyright © 1994 The Financial Training Co Ltd

ISBN 1 85179 614 2

Printed in England by Communications In Print plc, Basildon, Essex.

Contents

Introduction

This Central Assessment Pack is designed to prepare you for the central assessment set by the Association of Accounting Technicians (AAT) as part of their *Foundation* accounting course *(NVQ Level 2)*. It should be used in conjunction with the Study Packs published by the Financial Training Company.

The Central Assessment Pack consists of brief revision topics, followed by questions in the style of the central assessment model issued by the AAT. The sessions follow the same order as the Study Packs which cover these units.

Following Session 19, there is a *mock central assessment*, based on the AAT's own model, for you to attempt. The solution is *not* contained within the Central Assessment Pack.

PUBLISHER'S NOTE

Financial Training study materials are distributed in the UK and overseas by Stanley Thornes, (Publishers) Ltd. They are another company within the Wolters Kluwer group. They can be contacted at: Stanley Thornes, Ellenborough House, Wellington Street, Cheltenham GL50 1YD. Telephone: (0242) 228888. Fax: (0242) 221914.

Your chances of success in this course will be greatly improved by additional tuition, either at one of Financial Training's centres or by home study. For details of our open learning programmes, write or phone us at: Professional Studies, The Financial Training Company, 136-142 Bramley Road, London W10 6SR. Telephone: 081 960 4421. Fax: 081 960 9374.

We are always open to suggestions for improvements to our publications, including notification of any errors. Please send them directly to the Publishing Division, Financial Training at the above address.

Money and legal tender

REVISION TOPICS

Money may be held by a business in the forms of *cash* or *bank accounts*. Cash, comprising notes and coins, is held in small quantities so as to reduce the risk of theft.

Cash can be used as:

- a method of payment; or

- to buy postal orders, a method of payment which is used when it is unsafe to use cash, such as mailing a remittance.

A *bank current account* is used for day to day transactions, whereas a *bank deposit account* may be opened if the business has a surplus of funds in its current account.

The deposit account will earn interest, but there are restrictions on its use.

Payments can be made from current accounts to third parties using *cheques*, and cash, cheques and postal orders may be paid in, using a *paying-in slip* to summarise the details of the deposit. *Bank statements* are received by the business regularly, showing how money has gone into or left the bank account, and the amount of money held in the account after each days' transactions.

Legal tender is any method of payment which must be accepted *by law* in settlement of a debt. *Money* is anything which is generally acceptable as a method of settling a debt. Bank of England bank notes and £1 coins issued by the Royal Mint are *unlimited legal tender* in England, whereas other coins are *limited legal tender* with limits on the amount of currency which can be used as payment.

REVISION QUESTIONS

1   Give two examples of situations where a business will find it more convenient to use coins and notes rather than cheques.

2   Which of the following statements are generally true in respect of (a) bank current accounts and (b) bank deposit accounts?

(i)   A bank statement is received regularly.
(ii)   Cheques may be paid in to the account.
(iii)   Cheque payments may be made from the account.
(iv)   The account is useful for day to day transactions.
(v)   The account may be used as an investment, earning interest.

3   Jane Jones writes between 15 and 20 cheques each week. She deposits cash and cheques each Thursday; the number of cheques paid in varies between 4 and 9. She receives a bank statement on the first Wednesday of each month. Which of the following items will *not* appear on the bank statement received on 5th September?

(a)   Individual cheques paid in August.
(b)   Individual cheques received in August.
(c)   The balance on the account at the end of July.
(d)   The balance on the account at the end of August.

4   James Jenkins wishes to purchase a book entitled *Easy Money* by mail order. He has to send £5.15 in payment, but he does not have a bank account. Explain in detail how he may do this.

5   List the details on a cheque which have to be filled in by the account holder making a payment.

6   Janet Johnson wishes to settle her newspaper bill of £7.20 at the newsagents. Janet offers the newsagent the following alternatives in payment:

(a)   £7.20 in 10p pieces from a jar under her bed; or
(b)   £7 in £1 coins and 20p in 1p coins.

Can either alternative be used as legal tender?

Explain your answer.

Session 2

Receiving money in a credit business

REVISION TOPICS

All cash, cheques and postal orders received by a business are at risk of being lost or stolen, so should be:

- listed on a *remittance list*, then;

- locked in a safe or another secure place, then;

- banked at the earliest opportunity.

Security is improved if knowledge of the combination for the safe is restricted and the person banking the money is accompanied.

Customers paying immediately by cash or cheque are given a *receipt* to show that they have paid. Credit customers are given or sent an *invoice* showing the goods and services provided and the amount they must pay. A remittance advice is a slip returned by the customer with their payment so as to identify the invoice which is being paid.

Cash or settlement discounts are sometimes offered to credit customers to encourage them to pay more quickly and thus aid the cash flow of the business. A percentage reduction in the price charged is given if the customer pays within a certain period of time.

REVISION QUESTIONS

1   A cash discount of 3% is taken for early payment of an invoice for £84. How much cash is received in respect of this invoice?

2   £247.94 is received in respect of invoice 14303 to Brian Brainstorm Ltd. This company took advantage of a 2% settlement discount by paying within the 28-day time limit. What was the full amount of invoice 14303 before deduction of the discount?

3   Invoice 2714, for £110, is settled by Beth Brown within 30 days, thus qualifying for a $2^{1/2}\%$ cash discount. Assuming she takes advantage of the discount, show how this receipt would be recorded on the following remittance list:

REMITTANCES					
Customer	**Invoice No.**	**£**		**Discount allowed**	

4 List six errors that can be discovered when reviewing the remittance advices and cheques received.

5 What does E&OE printed on an invoice mean?

6 A cheque received from Ben Battersby for £1,350, in settlement of invoice H483 issued on 3 January 1994, has been dated 18 January 1993 rather than 18 January 1994. Consequently the cheque cannot be cashed. Write a letter to Mr Battersby requesting that the situation be rectified.

Making payments to credit suppliers

REVISION TOPICS

Payment by cheque is the best way to ensure that the correct person or business is paid. Security procedures for cheque payments include the following.

- The number of people authorised to sign cheques, *cheque signatories*, should be restricted.

- There should be two signatories for large amounts ie. exceeding a limit pre-set by the business.

- All payments should be supported by authorised documentation such as an invoice.

- Cheques should be used in strict numerical sequence.

- Unused (blank) cheques and cancelled cheques should be kept in a safe.

- There should be a segregation of duties between those who deal with suppliers' invoices, prepare the cheques and post the cheques.

A *remittance advice* will be sent with the cheque payment; these may be produced by the supplier with the invoice or by the business as part of a computerised cheque-printing run.

Tips and traps

Cash discounts may be received if payment is made within a time limit. If discounts are offered and VAT is included on the invoice

- *the discount is calculated on the net amount (excluding VAT)*

- *the VAT is calculated with reference to the discounted net amount, whether or not the discount is actually taken.*

REVISION QUESTIONS

1   List eight pieces of information which must appear on a full VAT invoice.

2   Anita Andrews receives an invoice for 10 cases of wine at £36 plus VAT at 17$1/2$% per case. The supplier, Fyne Wynes Ltd, offers no cash discounts. How much will Anita Andrews have to pay Fyne Wynes Ltd?

3   Aubrey Aitchinson buys six lorry tyres from Myers Tyres Ltd for £250 plus VAT at 17½%. Myers Tyres Ltd offers a settlement discount of 2% for payment within 28 days. How much will Aubrey Aitchinson have to pay Myers Tyres if payment is made;

(a)   within 28 days
(b)   after 28 days?

4   Today is 15 March and the following invoices are to be paid.

Invoice date	Supplier	Net amount before discount £	Discount available £	VAT at 17¹/2% £	Discount terms
20 February	Ambrose Ltd	431.24	10.78	73.58	30 days
1 March	Artgraphic	29.50	0.89	5.01	14 days
25 February	Andy's Autos	605.73	15.14	103.35	28 days

What are the total payments in respect of these invoices, assuming discounts are taken where appropriate?

5   How is control exercised over unused cheques?

6   Should spoiled cheques be destroyed?

Money in a retail business

REVISION TOPICS

A retailer will usually have a *till* or *cash register* which:

- stores cash for transactions and cheques, gift vouchers, book tokens and other forms of payment;

- records takings;

- issues sales receipts.

If the customer requests a VAT receipt and the transaction is below £100 including VAT at standard rate, retailers may issue a less detailed VAT receipt.

A *float* of coins and notes will be kept back when the takings in the till are banked so that change may be given to customers. Cash and cheques can be safely banked after the banks have closed by using the *nightsafe*; the retailer encloses two completed paying-in slips with the pouch of bankings and collects the stamped copy the next working day.

Customers paying by cheque should have a *cheque guarantee card*, guaranteeing a cheque up to the limit, usually £50, for that card. Only one cheque per transaction will be guaranteed. The retailer will check that

- the card is valid;

- details on the card and cheque agree;

- the cheque is signed in their presence and is correctly written and then write the card number on the reverse of the cheque.

Customers may pay by *credit card*.

- This method of payment is safe and convenient as there is no need to carry cash.

- Free credit is given – payments need only be made within 25 days of receiving a monthly payment.

- Payments can be spread out.

- After repaying part of their account, the customers can purchase more goods up to their credit limit again (*revolving credit*).

- Items bought can be taken away immediately.

The retailer will have to pay commission to the credit card company for each credit card payment, but often experiences increased sales as a result of offering the facility. Retailers also receive

- more security for payments in excess of £50; and

- immediate credit to their bank account of credit card vouchers paid in.

The credit card transaction is recorded on a *credit card sales voucher*. An *imprinter* is used to transfer the cardholder's and the retailer's details on the voucher and the transaction details are completed by the retailer.

The retailer checks that

- the card is valid;

- the number is not on a list of stolen cards;

- if the *floor limit* set by the credit card company is exceeded, their authorisation for the transaction will be given by telephone.

Credit card vouchers are banked using a *retail voucher summary*.

Many retailers use a computerised system of accepting credit cards. The technology is known as EFTPOS (Electronic Funds Transfer at Point of Sale). This authorises transactions electronically via a direct link between the retailer's terminal and the credit card company. *Debit cards* also use EFTPOS technology. These cards make payments direct from a bank account and there is no period of credit. *Storecards* are now offered by many retailers such as Laura Ashley and Marks and Spencer for use within their shops.

Retailers will have to refund payment if

- goods are faulty;

- goods are not as described;

- goods are not of merchantable quality;

- goods are not fit for the specific purpose for which they were sold; or

- the retailer agreed to do so in advance.

A sales receipt does not have to be produced by the customer for a refund. For credit card refunds, a *refund voucher* is completed and must be authorised by the credit card company if the original sale was authorised.

REVISION QUESTIONS

1   Chris Craggs buys some stationery from Ben's Pens and receives a receipt produced by a cash register. The receipt gives the following information:

- name, address and VAT registration number of Ben's Pens;

- date;

- date of supply;

- rate of VAT;

- brief description of the stationery bought;

- total amount payable including VAT at $17^{1}/_{2}\%$, being £54.

Chris Craggs requires a VAT receipt for his records. Will this receipt qualify?

2   Carol Collier wishes to pay for a new desk blotter costing £64. Which of the following methods of payment would be guaranteed by her £50 cheque guarantee card?

(a)   a cheque for £64;
(b)   a cheque for £50 and £14 cash;
(c)   a cheque for £50 and a cheque for £14.

3   Should the customer's name appear on

(a)   a completed credit card sales voucher;
(b)   a VAT invoice for £350 issued by a retailer;
(c)   a VAT invoice for £20 issued by a retailer;
(d)   a cheque guarantee card.

4   Charlie Cooper completes a retail voucher summary for credit card sales of £320 and refunds of £430. Which of the following is true?

(a)   He will write out a cheque to the credit card company for £430.
(b)   He will write out a cheque to the credit card company for £110.
(c)   He will not have to write out a cheque to the credit card company.

5   EFTPOS technology enables checking and authorisation to be performed by the credit card company's own computer. Is there anything that the retailer still has to check?

6   You are the proprietor of Ron's Records. One of your customers, Carl Crabbe, has written to you regarding some recent purchases. Below is an extract from the letter.

> 'One of the CDs you sold me has a big crack in it and won't play. Another one is described on the case as the London Symphony Orchestra playing 'The Nutcracker Suite', but when I opened it I found it was loud pop music by a group called The Cure. Also, I asked you for two tape cassettes suitable to play at the third birthday party of my daughter Carly. One seems suitable, but the other was a story for teenagers. I've changed my mind about these now and I'm going to show them a video, so I'd like my money back for all four items. I haven't got a receipt, but I know my rights.'

Write a letter to Mr Crabbe explaining his legal rights to a refund, referring to your policy of issuing a credit note if a refund is not legally required.

Services offered by the banks

REVISION TOPICS

Banks take deposits in current accounts and deposit accounts. They offer their customers money transfer services into and out of their account and can make advances in the forms of overdrafts, credit cards, loans, mortgages, business loans and credit card accounts. They also offer safe deposit boxes, nightsafes, foreign currency accounts, share-dealing, advice on investments, wills and insurance services.

Banks obtain payment for the customers when they pay in a cheque by crediting their account and then collecting the money from the third party. The *clearing system* takes three days and involves various physical transfers of the cheque as follows:

Day one	1	Cheques sorted at branch where paid in
	2	Sent to bank's own clearing department
Day two	3	Sent to central clearing house
	4	Sent to other bank's clearing department
Day three	5	Sent to branch of person who wrote cheque

If the accounts of the drawer and payee are at the same branch, the cheques do not need to leave the branch. If the accounts of the drawer and payee are at different branches of the same bank, steps 3 and 4 are omitted.

A *cheque* is an unconditional order in writing signed by the drawer, requiring a bank to pay on demand a sum certain in money to a named person or to the bearer.

When a cheque paid in by a customer has been accepted by a bank it must check:

- date (out of date after six months, post-dated, undated);

- payee's name;

- words and figures in agreement;

- signature present;

- crossings are obeyed;

- endorsements are consistent with the payee's name.

Endorsement of the back of a cheque by the payee allows it to be transferred to a third party.

Example – the payee is Mrs G Touchard

General   G Touchard, Mrs – payable to bearer

Specific   G Touchard, pay J Hobbs or order – payable to J Hobbs but may be reindorsed

Restrictive   G Touchard, pay to J Hobbs only

Cheque crossings mean that a cheque may be paid into a bank account only. A *special crossing* will detail the bank or branch into which the cheque must be paid. Pre-printed cheques have 'Account payee' printed on the crossing so that the cheque can only be paid into the account of the named payee and cannot be endorsed. Due to this, most forms of endorsement are now quite rare.

Other forms of payment include the following:

- *Bills of exchange* – the forerunner of cheques, today restricted mainly to trade with foreign countries.

- *Bankers draft* – a cheque drawn by a bank itself, useful when a bank's customer needs to pay a large sum of money (eg. to buy a house). It is the next best thing to money as it is guaranteed by the bank.

- *Standing orders* – an instruction to the bank to make regular payments, usually for fixed amounts at fixed intervals.

- *Direct debits* – an instruction to the bank to allow a third party to collect money from the customers' account, useful if the amount or payment dates can vary.

- *Bank giro credits* (credit transfers) – a means of transferring money from one account to another, useful for paying bills such as gas, electricity etc. and for paying wages. These payments are cleared through credit clearing which is similar to the cheque clearing system.

- *BACS* (Bankers Automated Clearing Services) – a method of clearing payments in which transactions are recorded on magnetic tape or discs and then processed at the BACS bureau rather than through the clearing house. It is used by banks for standing orders and companies for direct debits and salary payments.

- *CHAPS* (Clearing House Automated Payments System) is electronic clearing for large sums only.

REVISION QUESTIONS

1   Peter Parkin has an account at the Parliament Street, Nottingham branch of Lloyds Bank. He writes a cheque for £83 to Quentin Quaid who also has an account with Lloyds Bank, at their Church Lane, Worcester branch. Quentin pays the cheque in to his account.

       Describe how this cheque travels through the clearing system.

2   What is a general cheque endorsement and what is its function?

3   Will a cheque be honoured by a bank if the payee has:

    (a)   changed the date;

    (b)   written in the date as the drawer had not done so;

    (c)   repaired a cheque torn into two pieces by accident?

4   Pamela Poppins wishes to pay a cheque, made payable to Mr J and Mrs P Poppins, into an account in her sole name. Will the bank allow this?

5   What is the advantage to the employee of being paid their salary through BACS rather than by bank giro credit?

6   Would a cheque written out to pay 'My son £5,000 as long as I have £10,000 in my account' be valid?

Maintaining a cash book

REVISION TOPICS

A *cash book* records the receipts and payments into and out of the business' bank account, analysing each receipt and payment by type (an *analysed* cash book). The totals of each type of receipt and payment are *posted* each month to the general ledger by means of a journal entry, for example, if the cash book is purely a *book of prime entry*.

			£	£
Dr	Cash at bank (receipts)		800	
	Cr	Cash sales		300
	Cr	Debtors		447
	Cr	VAT		53
Dr	Creditors		530	
Dr	Rent		80	
Dr	Wages and salaries		100	
Dr	Insurance		40	
	Cr	Cash at bank (payments)		750
			1,550	1,550

Sometimes the cash book itself will be part of the double entry.

Cash discounts allowed or received are recorded in *memorandum columns* as a reminder to make the double entry in respect of discounts. The *actual amount paid or received* is recorded in the total and analysis columns.

A *bank reconciliation* is a control which is performed each month to ensure that the cash book has been correctly written up.

Tips and traps

Cash sales must have VAT analysed as this is the first time the sale has been recorded. Cash from debtors does not need to have VAT analysed as this is not the first time the sale has been recorded.

A credit in the cash book means a reduction in the bank balance. A credit on the bank statement means an increase in the bank balance as the statement of account is prepared from the bank's point of view. If you increase your bank balance, the bank is holding more of your money (ie. it owes you more), so their creditor is increased.

REVISION QUESTIONS

1   Show how the following payments are recorded on the extract from the cash book payments for 6 July given below:

   (a)   cash purchases of £45 + VAT at 17½%;

   (b)   cash paid to a creditor, Frank Field where the original sale was for £83 + VAT at 17½%;

   (c)   cash purchases of £27 including VAT at 17½% (work to the nearest pound).

Date	Narrative	Cheque No.	Total £	VAT £	Creditors £	Purchases £

2   What is a folio?

3   What is the double entry which records a settlement discount received of 2½% on payment of an invoice for purchases of £134 plus VAT at 17½%?

   Dr.................................... £............... Cr..................................... £...............

4   How much would be recorded in each of the following cash book receipts columns for a cash sale of £150 plus VAT at 17½% less a cash discount of 2%?

	£
Total	......
Cash sales	......
Debtors	......
VAT	......
Discounts allowed	......

5   A bank reconciliation is performed on 30 September 19X5 and the following reconciling items are found:

   •   deposits in transit   £23.50

   •   unpresented cheques   £8.43

   The bank statement shows a balance of £279.04. What is the balance in the cash book?

6   A trainee accounting technician, Freda Frith, is learning how to prepare a bank reconciliation and has given one to you to review. You notice that a standing order appears as a reconciling item along with deposits in transit and unpresented cheques. You are required to write a memorandum to Freda suggesting a more appropriate treatment of the standing order.

Banks and their customers

REVISION TOPICS

A *bank customer* is someone who has a current or similar account or who has agreed to open one. The bank may have a number of relationships with the customer:

- *Debtor/creditor relationship* as described below.

- *Principal* and *agent*

  The bank acts as agent for the principal (customer) when dealing with third parties eg. payment by direct debit.

- *Bailor* and *bailee*

  The bank acts as bailee by looking after the customer's (bailor's) property.

The bank agrees to hold, receive and collect customer's money and not to close the customer's account without reasonable notice. The customer agrees to take care in writing cheques and can only ask for repayment in writing.

The bank has a number of rights:

- to charge for services;

- to reclaim losses from customers;

- to exercise a *lien* over customer's property, ie. to keep goods as payment of debt;

- to use the customer's money as it wishes as long as it pays cheques written by customers; and

- to expect the customer to use reasonable care when writing cheques.

Its duties are as follows:

- to pay customer's cheques that are correctly completed by a customer who is not mentally incapacitated, bankrupt or dead!

- to obey express mandates such as standing orders

- to keep customer's details confidential

- to give reasonable notice of closure of an account

- to provide regular bank statements and to tell the customer the balance on their account on request

- to accept cash and cheques paid in by the customer

- to repay customer's money when the customer asks

- to tell the customer of any possible forgery of their signature

- to exercise proper skill and care – the customer trusts the bank and therefore the bank must act in an appropriate way (a fiduciary relationship)

The customer has a duty to use reasonable care when writing cheques and to tell the bank of any known forgery of his or her signature. The customer does *not* have to check the accuracy of his bank statement; the bank must be careful to ensure there are no mistakes.

REVISION QUESTIONS

1   You have an overdraft at the bank. Are you

    (a)   a customer of the bank?   Yes/No
    (b)   a creditor of the bank?   Yes/No
    (c)   a debtor of the bank?   Yes/No

2   In what capacity is the bank acting when holding valuable jewellery in a safe deposit box for a customer?

3   Who is responsible for ensuring that there are no errors on a bank account, the bank or the customer?

4   What is a lien? Illustrate your answer with an example.

5   List five duties of a bank.

6   Thomas Timms examined his bank statement for August 1994 and discovered that his account became overdrawn for two days whilst he was on holiday. Consequently he incurred bank charges for that month. He wrote to the bank complaining that his treatment had been unfair and the bank subsequently credited his account with the amount of the bank charges. Was the bank acting within its rights in making a charge for its services when Thomas Timms was overdrawn? Explain your answer.

Petty cash

REVISION TOPICS

Petty cash is used to make small cash payments. The cash is obtained by cashing a cheque at the bank or from cash sales. Payments are recorded on a numbered voucher and require authorisation prior to the money being paid. Receipts are attached to the voucher.

Payments are also recorded in the petty cash book which analyses the expenses paid for and VAT if the business can reclaim it.

An *imprest system* is often used as it reduces the risk of theft or fraud. This operates by topping up the petty cash to a pre-set level each week. This level will be based on the requirements of the business. As each petty cash payment is made, a voucher for that value will be completed such that:

cash + vouchers = original amount of cash

At the end of the week, the petty cashier is reimbursed for the value of the vouchers which are filed.

REVISION QUESTIONS

1   Dave Danvers keeps a petty cash imprest of £100. On Monday 5 January the petty cash box contains vouchers totalling £25. How much cash is in the petty cash box?

2   List five items which would generally appear on a petty cash voucher.

3   The following totals from the petty cash book were obtained at the end of a week's trading:

			£	£
Debits	Cheque cashed at bank		135	
	Credits	Postage		23
		Cleaning		18
		Refreshments		52
		Newspapers		12
		VAT		12
			135	117

The imprest level is £150. What journal entry will be made for this week to record petty cash payments in the general ledger?

4   Which of the following payments would generally not be made through petty cash?

   (a)   Wages for casual labour of £28
   (b)   Window cleaning of £9.50
   (c)   Milk bill of £38

5   What would be the double entry recording the cashing of a cheque for £72 from the business's bank account to top up the petty cash?

   Dr.. Cr..

6   Your friend Daniel Dawson has sought your advice regarding the cash payments of his car repair business which is expanding rapidly. His cash payments had been about £10 per week but have now increased to around £100 per week as he has taken on new staff and moved from his back garden to small commercial premises. He says he finds it difficult to keep track of all the cash he spends on coffee, tea and other consumables and often feels he is out of pocket.

   Write a letter to him, briefly describing how he might set up and operate a petty cash imprest system which will be under his sole control, due to the size of the business.

Trading on credit terms

REVISION TOPICS

It is important for a business to operate controls over credit sales to ensure that they will receive cash from their customers in the period of credit agreed in their contract. With *new* customers, *trade references, bank references* and references from *agencies* such as Dun and Bradstreet will be investigated to establish their creditworthiness. A *credit limit* will then be set for that customer. Established customers will constantly be reviewed to ensure that they are paying outstanding invoices on a timely basis and that their credit limit will not be exceeded by new orders. Credit limits should be reviewed regularly and a *stop list* used to prevent goods and services from being supplied to customers identified as risky.

The customer will initiate a credit transaction by sending a *purchase order* for the goods they require. The business will confirm this order by raising a *sales order* which also serves to prompt the purchase or manufacture of the goods. A sequentially-numbered *delivery note* or *despatch note*, signed by the customer, advises them of the goods delivered and is used internally to update stock records and initiate invoicing. A *sales invoice* showing the quantity of goods supplied and the amount to be paid is sent to the customer. Sales invoices should be:

- sequentially-numbered;

- used in order, keeping spoiled copies;

- checked to ensure that all deliveries and only proper deliveries are invoiced;

- authorised before being sent to customers; and

- correctly coded as to customer account and product type to ensure correct recording in the ledgers.

Trade or bulk discounts may be given to certain customers depending on the level of goods or services they guarantee to buy. VAT is calculated *after* deduction of the discount which is shown on the invoice.

REVISION QUESTIONS

1   A delivery note is produced in a four-part set. Suggest how each copy will be used.

2   A car spares distributor has a warehouse which stores exhaust pipes. Each month, the number of exhaust pipes of each type despatched is calculated from the delivery notes at the warehouse. The sales invoicing department at the head office perform a similar calculation using their copies of sales invoices. The totals are then compared and discrepancies investigated.

This is an example of the use of .... as a means of checking that all deliveries and only genuine deliveries are invoiced.

3   For all orders of 1,000 items, James' Games Ltd offers a discount of 1%, thereafter increasing by $1/2$% for every 250.

If 1,750 items are ordered at £1 each plus VAT at $17^1/2$%, what will be the total invoice value?

4   On a VAT invoice, the date of supply of goods is called the ....? If the invoice is made out after the date of supply the date is called the ....?

5   If a price quoted on an invoice is 'ex works' what does this mean to the customer?

6   What is a stop list?

Maintaining the sales day book

REVISION TOPICS

The *sales day book* is a diary of all credit sales invoices in numerical and date order, prepared from the invoices and recording customer code and product code. The invoice totals are analysed by product and the VAT element is separated out to give the true sales value to the business of each product.

Tips and traps

*The **totals** for each product and VAT are posted to the general ledger using a journal entry.*

Example

			£	£
Dr	*Debtors ledger control account*		*X*	
	Cr	*Sales – product A*		*X*
		Sales – product B		*X*
		VAT control account		*X*

Credit sales for the week ending 13 March 1994.

There are several different systems of coding:

* sequential
* block (allocates bands of numbers to particular categories)
* significant digit (individual digits and letters used to represent features of the coded item)
* decimal/hierarchical (eg. 3 = social science, 37 = education, etc.)

Accounting systems may be manual or computerised. They basically work in the same way.

There are two methods of processing:

* batch processing (large numbers of transactions are grouped together and processed at the same time)

* on-line, real-time processing (transactions are input as they occur)

A *file* is an organised collection of individual *records* which share a common structure. A *field* is a section of a *record*. Each field contains a single item of information. A *character* is a unit which is a letter, number or symbol making up a field.

REVISION QUESTIONS

1   Which of the following best describes a sales day book?

    (a)   A ledger
    (b)   A journal
    (c)   A book of prime entry

2   What is the double entry to record sales of £700 plus VAT at the standard rate in the general ledger?

3   The managing director of Able Tables Ltd is concerned about the number of errors the auditors found in the posting of the general ledger from the sales day book. At present the sales day book is written up and the journal entry voucher prepared by Jonathan Owen, a clerk. There appear to be no errors in the sales daybook. Jonathan then passes the journal entry to Oliver Johnson who inputs all the journal vouchers to the computerised accounting system. Oliver Johnson has not been known to make mistakes in posting journal vouchers from other sources. The managing director has asked you, the accountant, to suggest how to ensure that posting of credit sales is more reliable. Write a memorandum to the managing director, Janice Oswald, regarding this matter.

4   Why should the sales department be prevented from setting credit limits for new customers?

5   From which of the following is the sales day book written up?

    (a)   Sales orders
    (b)   Sales invoices

6   Which of the following invoice details are not usually found in the sales day book?

    (a)   Customer name
    (b)   Customer address
    (c)   Total payable
    (d)   Discount allowed

7   In a computerised accounting system:

    (a)   The sales ledger will be a:

           file / record / field

    (b)   The amount owed by a particular customer will be a:

           file / record / field

    (c)   The account details of a particular customer will be a:

           file / record / field

8   Give *two* advantages of batch processing.

Maintaining the debtors' ledger

REVISION TOPICS

The *debtors' ledger* or *sales ledger* is separate from the nominal ledger. It contains an account for each individual customer and shows the amounts owed by and all transactions with each customer.

The debtors' ledger is compiled mainly from:

* the sales day book which gives details of individual invoices

* the cash book which details cash received from and discounts allowed to each customer

Other entries on accounts in the debtors' ledger include *bad debts* written off, *contras* and correction of errors.

The *debtors' ledger control account* or *sales ledger control account* is in the nominal ledger and records the total amount outstanding from debtors. A *debtors' ledger reconciliation* is a control performed regularly to ensure that the debtors ledger and debtors' ledger control account record the same total amount outstanding for debtors. The total of a list of balances compiled from the debtors ledger is compared with the balance on the debtors' ledger control account and any discrepancies are investigated and adjusted for appropriately.

Tips and traps

*Individual invoices and cash receipts are recorded in the debtors' ledger which acts as a memorandum of amounts owed. **Totals** of sales and cash receipts are recorded in the debtors' ledger control account in the nominal ledger.*

Debtors are recorded at the gross sales value, including VAT, as this is what they have to pay.

REVISION QUESTIONS

1   In an individual account in the debtors' ledger, is a cash receipt recorded on the debit or credit side?

2   What document is usually used to match cash receipts to individual invoices?

   (a)   Remittance advice
   (b)   Paying-in slip
   (c)   Despatch note

3   William Walker's balance in the debtors' ledger is cancelled with part of his balance in the creditors' ledger with his agreement. This is an example of a ....

4   A discount of £20 allowed to the customer, Wanda Wright, was recorded in the cash book and subsequently treated as a discount received.

What adjustments for this are required:

(a)   in the nominal ledger; and
(b)   in the debtors' ledger?

5   Which of the following errors discovered during the performance of a debtors ledger reconciliation will require adjustment in the debtors' ledger?

(a)	Sales day book incorrectly cast	Yes/No
(b)	Individual invoice amount incorrectly recorded in sales day book	Yes/No
(c)	Discount received not recorded anywhere in the cash book	Yes/No
(d)	Bad debt written off recorded only in the nominal ledger	Yes/No

6   The following information is relevant for October 1994:

	£
Balance on debtors' ledger control account, 1 October	3,750
Invoices issued for credit sales	12,632
Invoices received for purchases	8,929
Cash received from debtors	13,004
Cash sales	2,120
Bad debts written off	1,200
Cash paid to suppliers	7,768

What is the balance on the debtors' ledger control account on 31 October 1994?

BOOKKEEPING EXERCISE

The tasks in this exercise are all based on the transactions of a medium-sized wholesale company.

Data

The following transactions all occurred on 1 March 19X4 and have been entered for you into summarised books of original entry. (VAT has in this instance been calculated to the nearest £.)

Treat 'other customers' as an individual account.

Sales day book

	Total £	VAT £	Net £
Allardyce & Sons	3,419	510	2,909
Edward Prior & Co	2,356	351	2,005
Chetwynd Bros	5,578	830	4,748
Rothman Stores	1,633	243	1,390
Bluntishall Supplies Ltd	13,769	2,050	11,719
Robertson Productions Ltd	11,257	1,676	9,581
Yew Tree Merchants Ltd	957	143	814
Thomas Allfarthing & Co	2,917	434	2,483
Drewitt & Sons	109	17	92
Peartree Manufacturing	266	39	227
Bradley Bros	6,838	1,020	5,818
Other customers	16,323	2,431	13,892
	65,422	9,744	55,678

Journal

		Debit £	Credit £
Dr	Bad debts	222	
	Cr Debtors' control account		222

Being Finch & Co written off (included in other customers)

		Debit £	Credit £
Dr	Creditors' control account	873	
	Cr Debtors' control account		873

Being a contra with the creditors ledger (Chetwynd Bros)

Cash book

	Discount £	Net receipt £
Receipts		
Edward Prior & Co	92	4,539
Chetwynd Bros	66	3,254
Robertson Productions Ltd	82	4,051
	240	11,844

The following are selected balances only at the start of the day on 1 March 19X4:

	£
Customers	
Allardyce & Sons	9,143
Edward Prior & Co	8,763
Chetwynd Bros	6,036
Rothman Stores	10,475
Bluntishall Supplies Ltd	29,669
Robertson Productions Ltd	20,243
Yew Tree Merchants Ltd	–
Thomas Allfarthing & Co	278,351
Drewitt & Sons	685
Peartree Manufacturing	4,335
Bradley Bros	18,286
Other customers	404,628
Other	
Sales	2,203,622
VAT (credit balance)	35,883
Debtors control account	790,614

Complete all the following tasks

Tasks

(1)   Enter the opening balances into the following accounts:

Debtors' control account
Sales
VAT
Edward Prior & Co
Chetwynd Bros
Robertson Productions Ltd

Use the working paper provided.

(2)   Enter all relevant transactions into the accounts shown in task (1).

(3)   Balance off all the accounts in which you have made entries in task (2).

(4)   Calculate the closing balances of the remaining customer accounts and complete the list of balances. Use the working paper provided.

(5)   Reconcile the closing balance of the debtors' control account to the total of the list of closing customer balances prepared in task (4).

GENERAL LEDGER

Debtors' Control Account

Date	Details	Amount £	Date	Details	Amount £

Sales

Date	Details	Amount £	Date	Details	Amount £

VAT

Date	Details	Amount £	Date	Details	Amount £

DEBTORS' LEDGER

Edward Prior & Co

Date	Details	Amount £	Date	Details	Amount £

Chetwynd Bros

Date	Details	Amount £	Date	Details	Amount £

Robertson Productions Ltd

Date	Details	Amount £	Date	Details	Amount £

	£	£

Updated debtors' control account balance

_____

Updated customer balances:

	£
Allardyce & Sons	_____
Edward Prior & Co	_____
Chetwynd Bros	_____
Rothman Stores	_____
Bluntishall Supplies Ltd	_____
Robertson Productions Ltd	_____
Yew Tree Merchants Ltd	_____
Thomas Allfarthing & Co	_____
Drewitt & Sons	_____
Peartree Manufacturing	_____
Bradley Bros	_____
Other customers	_____

Total updated customer balances

_____

Sales returns and credit notes

REVISION TOPICS

A *credit note* is issued by a supplier to cancel all or part of a previous sale. The customer may either have returned the goods or not received all the goods invoiced and requires a *refund*. In some cases a credit note is issued to settle a *dispute*. Credit notes cannot be issued to cancel a bad debt and thereby recover the VAT.

A *returns inwards* note will be raised to record returned goods received by the supplier and this will be used to initiate the credit note which must be authorised prior to issue. Written authorisation is required for the issue of credit notes not relating to returned goods.

Credit notes are recorded in a *sales returns day book* and this is posted in the same way as the sales day book.

REVISION QUESTIONS

1   Which of the following could give rise to a credit or negative balance on a customer's account in the debtors ledger?

(a)	A credit note being issued after the customer has paid	Yes/No
(b)	A customer paying cash in excess of invoices outstanding	Yes/No
(c)	An amount outstanding being written off as a bad debt	Yes/No
(d)	A credit note being recorded in the wrong account	Yes/No

2   List four reasons why a credit note would be issued.

3   Which of the following pieces of information need not be shown on a credit note produced by a business registered for VAT?

(a)	Original invoice number	Yes/No
(b)	Reason for issue	Yes/No
(c)	Date of issue	Yes/No
(d)	Supplier's VAT registration number	Yes/No
(e)	Customer's VAT registration number	Yes/No
(f)	Customer's name and address	Yes/No

4   What document/book of prime entry is used to prepare the journal entry recording credit notes in the nominal ledger:

returns inwards note/sales returns day book/credit note?

5   When posting individual credit notes from the sales returns daybook to the debtor's ledger, two mistakes are made:

(a)   a credit note for £240 is debited to the account of Gleam Cleaners Ltd; and

(b)   a credit note for £84 is credited to the account of Bright Lights Ltd instead of Cool Shades & Co.

What action is required in respect of these errors?

6   Mr Moss, the finance director, has requested a review of procedures for issuing credit notes. You have concluded that more stringent checks are required prior to authorisation of credit notes. At present the sales manager checks the current price lists to ensure that the prices credited are correct and checks the details of price, quantity and customer on the returns inwards note.

Write a report to the finance director suggesting further checks to be performed by the sales manager.

BOOKKEEPING EXERCISE

Data

The following transactions all occurred on 1 April 19X5 and have been entered for you into summarised books of original entry.

Treat 'other customers' as an individual account.

Sales day book

	Total £	VAT £	Net £
Garnett Ltd	4,413	657	3,756
Wells Stores	3,447	513	2,934
Lawrence & Sons	6,377	950	5,427
Shields Ltd	2,791	416	2,375
Nicolson Partnership	34,950	5,205	29,745
Grenfell Bros	11,549	1,720	9,829
Malory Homecare Ltd	3,957	589	3,368
Nesbit Ltd	1,000	149	851
Other customers	27,883	4,153	23,730
	96,367	14,352	82,015

Sales returns day book

	Total £	VAT £	Net £
Wells Stores	112	17	95
Nicolson Partnership	3,725	555	3,170
Grenfell Bros	284	42	242
	4,121	614	3,507

Journal

		Debit £	Credit £
Dr	Office expenses	31	
	Cr Telephone		31

Being the correction of an error made on 15 March 19X5

Cash book

			£
Opening balance at start of day			2,502 (debit)

Receipts	*Discount* £	*Net receipt* £	
Wells Stores	105	5,237	
Lawrence & Sons	62	3,069	
Grenfell Bros	96	4,794	
Nesbit Ltd	48	2,397	
	311		15,497

Payments		
Cash purchases (including VAT at 17.5%)	800	
Office expenses	945	
Interest	86	
Transfers to petty cash	100	
		(1,931)
Closing balance at end of day		16,068 (debit)

Petty cash book

	£
Balance at start of day	55
Receipts – transfers from bank account	100
Payments – office expenses (including VAT at 17.5%)	(47)
Balance at end of day	108

Nominal ledger balances at the start of the day on 1 April 19X5

	£
Customers	
Garnet Ltd	9,423
Wells Stores	8,077
Lawrence & Sons	6,598
Shields Ltd	8,614
Nicolson Partnership	37,983
Grenfell Bros	29,514
Malory Homecare Ltd	–
Nesbit Ltd	1,702
Other customers	378,955
Others	
Purchases	2,647,883
Sales	3,114,304
Sales returns	6,358
Telephone	734
Office expenses	8,595
Interest	1,211
VAT	33,732 (credit)
Debtors' control account	480,866
Creditors' control account	307,332
Discounts allowed	15,898
Other debit balances	808,140
Other credit balances	516,874

Complete all the following tasks

Tasks

(1)   Enter the opening balances into the following accounts:

   Debtors' control account
   Office expenses
   Sales
   VAT
   Wells Stores
   Lawrence & Sons
   Grenfell Bros

   Use the working papers provided.

(2)   Enter all relevant transactions into the accounts shown in task (1).

(3)   Balance off all the accounts in which you have made entries in task (2).

(4)   Calculate the closing balances of the remaining customer accounts and complete the list of balances.

(5)   Reconcile the closing balance of the debtors' control account to the total of the list of closing customer balances.

(6)   Calculate the closing balances of the remaining accounts. Complete the list of balances by inserting the updated figures for each account in either the debit balances column or the

credit balances column as appropriate. Total the two columns. The two totals should be the same. If they do not agree, try to trace and correct any errors you have made within the time you have available.

GENERAL LEDGER

Debtors' control account

Date	Details	Amount £	Date	Details	Amount £

Office expenses

Date	Details	Amount £	Date	Details	Amount £

Sales

Date	Details	Amount £	Date	Details	Amount £

VAT

Date	Details	Amount £	Date	Details	Amount £

DEBTORS' LEDGER

Wells Stores

Date	Details	Amount £	Date	Details	Amount £

Lawrence & Sons

Date	Details	Amount £	Date	Details	Amount £

Grenfell Bros

Date	Details	Amount £	Date	Details	Amount £

	£	£

Updated debtors' control account balance

Updated customer balances:

Garnett Ltd

Wells Stores

Lawrence & Sons

Shields Ltd

Nicolson Partnership

Grenfell Bros

Malory Homecare Ltd

Nesbit Ltd

Other customers

Total updated customer balances

List of updated balances at the end of the day on 1 April 19X5:

	Debit £	Credit £
Purchases		
Sales		
Sales returns		
Telephone		
Office expenses		
Interest		
VAT		
Debtors' control account		
Creditors' control account		
Discounts allowed		
Bank		
Petty cash		
Other debit balances	808,140	
Other credit balances		516,874

Using information to control debtors

REVISION TOPICS

An *aged analysis of debtors*, prepared from the debtor's ledger, shows the age of debts. The *credit controller* uses this to identify and chase up old unpaid invoices. *Statements* of unpaid invoices are produced each month and sent to the customers. This serves as a reminder to the customer and as an internal control to the supplier as it may reveal errors in the debtor's ledger.

The credit controller chases payment by means of telephone or letter, but will resort to the courts if the customer refuses to pay and has no complaints about the goods or services received.

REVISION QUESTIONS

1   Which of the following documents are sent to customers?

(a)	Invoice	Yes/No
(b)	Returns inwards note	Yes/No
(c)	Supplier's statement	Yes/No
(d)	Aged analysis of debtors	Yes/No
(e)	Credit note	Yes/No

2   Today is 30 June 19X5. Prepare an aged analysis of Farden's Garden Supplies using details from their account below.

FARDEN'S GARDEN SUPPLIES					F1
Date		**£**	**Date**		**£**
15.2.X5	Invoice 3397	224.36	28.3.X5	Cheque	333.58
20.2.X5	Invoice 3408	109.22	25.4.X5	Cheque	470.19
4.3.X5	Invoice 3470	24.89	23.5.X5	Credit note 143	44.00
18.3.X5	Invoice 3521	321.50			
20.4.X5	Invoice 3604	148.69			
24.4.X5	Invoice 3643	76.40			
18.5.X5	Invoice 3712	129.53			
19.5.X5	Invoice 3728	44.00			
3.6.X5	Invoice 3794	148.36			
16.6.X5	Invoice 3862	15.04			

3   The diagram below shows part of the organisational structure of Bogo's Pogos Ltd.

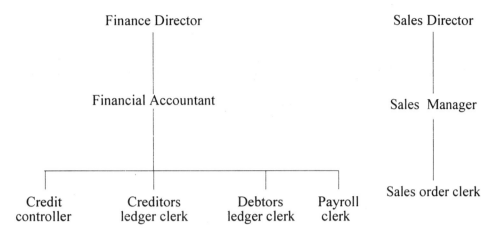

Whose job is it to

(a)   prepare statements to send to debtors;
(b)   prepare aged debtor's listing;
(c)   review aged debtor's listing;
(d)   review credit notes; and
(e)   contact the customer regarding unpaid debts?

4   How can a supplier's statement which is sent to an external customer act as an internal control?

5   Most businesses trading on credit offer a 30-day period in which payment should be made.

(a)   Why are discounts offered for payment within this period?

(b)   Why are customers not taken to court immediately after the 30-day period if bills are still unpaid?

6   You have received a letter from Bone's Phones, a customer, complaining that their recent statement for 28 February 19X3 did not agree with their records. There were two discrepancies:

(a)   a cheque for £430 sent by Bone's Phones on 26 February was not received by you until 1 March; and

(b)   Bone's Phones insist that a disputed invoice, numbered H413, relates to goods which were never received.

The goods referred to in (b) have now been found on the premises of a different customer and a credit note authorised in respect of invoice H413.

Write a letter to Mr Bone of Bone's Phones explaining the discrepancies.

Legal relationship of buyer and seller

REVISION TOPICS

A *contract* is a legally binding agreement which can be enforced by the courts under civil law. A contract has seven fundamental requirements in order to be valid:

- agreement (= offer and acceptance);

- the intention to create legal relations;

- consideration;

- written formalities (some contracts only);

- capacity to contract;

- genuine consent; and

- the contract must be legal and possible.

A contract declared *void* means that neither party may enforce any rights under the contract and money or goods handed over must be returned. This could occur, for example, if some fundamental mistake concerning the contract has been made.

If one of the parties may avoid the contract at their option (for example, if some fact relating to the contract was misrepresented to him) it is *voidable* and anything which happens before the contract is avoided is valid.

An unenforceable contract is valid in theory but due to the lack of some legal formality or evidence it cannot be sued upon or enforced by the court.

Agreement between the parties requires an *offer* made by the offeror to be *accepted* by the other party, the offeree. The offer is an expression of willingness to contract on certain terms with the intention that it will become binding if accepted by the other party. An offer must be communicated to the offeree and may be:

- made to a specific person or the world at large;

- conditional, but it must be certain; and

- express or implied.

An offer should not be confused with an *invitation to treat* which is an invitation made by the first party to a second party to make an offer to the first party. Acceptance should be made whilst the offer is still in force and be absolute and unqualified, otherwise a counter offer will be made. Acceptance must be communicated to the offeror where notification is specifically or tacitly required.

Once an offer *lapses*, it cannot be accepted. An offer may be *revoked* (or withdrawn) by the offeror at any time before it has been accepted. The offeree may notify the offeror that he does not wish to accept the offer. Rejection may be express or implied.

There should be an intention to create legal relations if an agreement is to become a contract. This is presumed in commercial agreements, but not in domestic or social arrangements.

Contracts may be made informally, even verbally, except in cases where they must be:

- made by deed, eg. where there is no consideration as in a 'deed of gift' to charity, contracts for the transfer of a British registered ship or aeroplane and legal conveyances of land or leases of land for more than three years;

- in writing, eg. transfer of company shares, bills of exchange and cheques, hire purchase contracts, contracts of marine insurance and contracts for the future sale of interests in land; or

- evidenced in writing, eg. money-lending agreements and contracts of guarantee.

Minors (persons under 18) do not have the capacity to enter into any contract that they wish. They may enter into contracts for 'necessaries' or contracts which benefit them (eg. contracts for education). Most contracts other than these are *unenforceable* by the third party against the minor, but enforceable by the minor against the third party.

The parties to a contract must have genuinely consented to its terms. The genuineness of the consent will be affected if *mistake* or *misrepresentation* has occurred.

REVISION QUESTIONS

1   The law of contract is a branch of:

   (a)   common law;
   (b)   criminal law;
   (c)   civil law?

2   Freda Fynnes discovers a dress in her local boutique priced at £39. Freda takes the dress to the proprietor who says that the dress has the wrong price tag on it and that she can buy it for the real price of £59. Freda insists that she should be allowed to buy the dress for £39 as she has accepted the proprietor's offer to sell it at this price. Is Freda correct? Explain your answer briefly.

3   Fred, who lives in Aberystwyth, offers to sell his car to his friend, William, who lives in Bath, for £2,400. Fred says that William must make up his mind before Friday at 5 p.m. when his other friend, Phil is coming to look at it with a view to buying it. William posts his acceptance of the offer to Fred on Thursday, but Fred does not receive the letter until Saturday morning, by which time Fred has sold the car to Phil. Can William sue Fred for breach of contract?

4   Mr and Mrs Wright live in a large detached house with a sizeable garden and have an informal agreement that Mr Wright should do the gardening and Mrs Wright should do the washing and ironing. They employ Mrs Scrubbitt who has agreed to perform a schedule of housework and is paid at a commercial rate for domestic work.

Is there a contract between:

(a)   Mr and Mrs Wright; and
(b)   the Wrights and Mrs Scrubbitt?

Explain your answer briefly.

5   Which of the following contracts must be in writing?

(a)	Transfer of shares in a limited company	Yes/No
(b)	Transfer of a British registered ship	Yes/No
(c)	A loan of money from a finance company	Yes/No

6   A valid contract requires consideration. What does this mean? Illustrate your answer with a simple example.

Receiving purchase invoices

REVISION TOPICS

A *purchase requisition* is an internal document used to request goods and services. The buying department then raises a sequentially-numbered *purchase order* to confirm an order with the supplier. This must be authorised by the relevant department head, unless the amount of the order exceeds his or her authorisation limit in which case a director should authorise it.

A goods received note is used to record all incoming goods which will be accompanied by the supplier's delivery note.

On receipt the *purchase invoice* is checked by the purchase ledger clerk:

- for accuracy of pricing, VAT and discounts;

- for clerical accuracy;

- to the purchase order; and

- to the goods received note and despatch note.

The clerk will date stamp the invoice, give it a sequential number and record it in a *purchase invoice register*. It is then sent for coding and authorisation by the relevant department head and the clerk will record it in the *purchase day book*.

VAT on purchases may be reclaimed if both the business and supplier are registered for VAT, the expenditure is not disallowable and the business has a proper VAT invoice.

REVISION QUESTIONS

1   A purchase requisition is received by the buying department. What document will they raise in response?

2   How is a goods received note useful in the exercise of internal control?

3   Purchase invoices are stamped on receipt with the grid to be completed – for internal use. What details usually need to be completed on the grid?

4   How can control be exercised over the payment of invoices for services if there is no goods received note or delivery note?

5   When can VAT be reclaimed on purchases?

6   Crackpotts and Co order and receive 30 novelty teapots at £12 each from their supplier, Madhatter and Mouse Ltd. However, the purchase invoice received from Madhatter and Mouse Ltd is for 35 teapots. You are Alice White, the creditors ledger clerk and you discover this when checking the purchase invoice, goods received note and purchase order. Write a letter to the supplier requesting a credit note for the additional five teapots invoiced.

Maintaining the purchase day book

REVISION TOPICS

The *purchase day book* is a diary of all credit transactions, recording each purchase invoice. The purchases are analysed by type of product or service excluding VAT where it is recoverable; a separate VAT column is used where it is recoverable.

The purchase day book is posted at regular intervals using a journal entry such as:

				£	£
Debit:	Purchases	–	Product 1	500.00	
		–	Product 2	320.00	
		–	Product 3	100.00	
	Electricity			85.00	
	Rent			220.00	
	Stationery			30.00	
	VAT control			181.13	
Credit:	Creditors ledger control account				1,436.13

REVISION QUESTIONS

1   Which of the following would not be detailed in the purchase day book?

(a)	Recoverable VAT		Yes/No
(b)	Irrecoverable VAT		Yes/No
(c)	Discount received		Yes/No
(d)	Discount allowed		Yes/No
(e)	Cash purchases		Yes/No

2   Transfer the following invoice details into the purchase day book below, allocating appropriate dates, invoice numbers and supplier details.

(a)   Three girls' dresses (code 01) at £9 each (no VAT on children's clothing)
(b)   Five ladies dresses (code 02) at £27 plus VAT each
(c)   Catering for customer's open evening (code 04) £430 plus VAT (disallowable)

Date	Invoice No.	Code	Supplier	Total £	VAT £	01 £	02 £	03 £	04 £

3   What is the journal entry to post the following totals from the purchase day book to the general ledger?

		£
Raw materials	– steel	2,439
	– wood	751
Components		203
Sundries		76
Sub contractors		600
Electricity		185
Fixed assets – car		14,000
VAT		745
Total		18,999

4   Both the purchase invoice register and the purchase day book should list all purchase invoices received for credit transactions.

Is this statement true?

5   What function does the purchase invoice register serve?

6   Why does a business allocate its own number to a purchase invoice when it will already have a supplier's invoice number?

Maintaining the creditors ledger

REVISION TOPICS

The *creditors ledger* or *purchase ledger* is separate from the nominal ledger. It contains an account for each individual supplier and shows the amounts owed to, and all transactions with, each supplier. It is compiled mainly from:

- the purchase day book which gives details of individual invoices; and

- the cash book which details cash payments to and discounts received from each supplier.

Contras and *adjustments* for the correction of errors will also be found in the creditor's ledger accounts.

The *creditors ledger control account* or *purchase ledger control account* is in the nominal ledger and records the total amount owing to creditors. A *creditors ledger reconciliation* is a control performed regularly to ensure that the creditors ledger and creditors ledger control account record the same total amount owing to creditors. The total of a list of balances compiled from the creditors ledger is compared with the balance on the creditor's ledger control account and any differences are investigated and adjusted for appropriately.

Tips and traps

*Individual invoices and cash payments are recorded in the creditors ledger which acts as a memorandum of amounts owed. **Totals** of sales and cash payments are recorded in the creditor's ledger control account in the nominal ledger.*

Creditors are recorded at the gross amount, including VAT, as this is what has to be paid.

REVISION QUESTIONS

1   In which ledgers would you find the following accounts?

    (a)   Creditor's ledger control account
    (b)   Ken Kimberly, supplier
    (c)   Keith Kemp, customer
    (d)   Discounts received

2   Is discount received a debit or credit entry in a creditor's individual account?

3   An invoice received from Karen Krebs wholesale stationery supplies is for two boxes of 200 window envelopes at £7.50 plus standard rated VAT per box. How much will be recorded in Karen Krebs' creditor's ledger account in respect of this invoice?

4   Classify the accounts listed below as an asset, a liability, an expense or income:

     (a)   Creditors ledger control account
     (b)   Discounts received
     (c)   Light and heat
     (d)   Balance at bank

5   When extracting the creditors ledger balances onto the list for reconciliation with the creditors ledger control account, two errors were made:

     (a)   a debit balance of £430 was listed as a credit balance; and
     (b)   a balance of £620 was omitted.

     The total of the list of balances before adjusting for the items above was £4,966. What is the corrected total?

6   You have been consulted by letter from Charlie Harley who runs a small, but growing, manufacturing business. He wishes to keep a tighter control over the recording of payments to suppliers and has asked you to explain how to perform a creditor's ledger reconciliation. His creditor's ledger clerk, John Conn, will perform the reconciliation as Charlie does not have time.

     Write a letter to Charlie Harley explaining how the creditors ledger reconciliation is performed and suggest how the control could be improved given that the creditor's ledger clerk will carry out the reconciliation.

BOOKKEEPING EXERCISE

The tasks in this exercise are based on the transactions of a wholesaling company. The transactions which took place during the month of May 19X5 have been summarised and reproduced below.

At 1 May 19X5 the balances in the general ledger, the debtors' ledger and the creditors' ledger are as shown in the accounts on the attached ledger working sheets.

Treat 'other customers' and 'other suppliers' as individual accounts.

Data

Credit sales for May

	Total £	VAT £	Net £
Willowes Ltd	627	94	533
Howard & Howard	360	54	306
Chapman Ltd	729	108	621
Other customers	43,394	6,463	36,931
	45,110	6,719	38,391

Credit purchases for May

	Total £	VAT £	Net £	Goods for resale £	Other items £
Atwood & Co	5,730	853	4,877	4,877	
Karlin & Partners	4,455	656	3,799	3,799	
Hardy Ltd	2,082	310	1,772	1,772	
Other suppliers	14,788	2,202	12,586	8,528	4,058
	27,055	4,021	23,034	18,976	4,058

Analysis of other items purchased

	£
Telephones	566
Repairs and renewals	910
Postage and stationery	476
Travel and subsistence	306
Other expenditure	1,800
	4,058

Bank current account for May

1 May 19X5   Opening balance   32,642 (debit)

Receipts:

	Cash discount £	Net amount received £
Willowes Ltd		435
Howard & Howard		371
Chapman Ltd	16	452
Beaumann & Baker		251
Other customers	102	34,633
	118	36,142

Payments:

	Cash discount £	Net amount received £
Atwood & Co		4,069
Karlin & Partners	87	3,415
Hardy Ltd		2,418
Other suppliers	134	14,237
	221	24,139
Wages and salaries – May		9,151
Customs and Excise – VAT		8,061
Petty cash		39
	221	41,390

Petty cash summary – May

	£
Balance – 1 May	21
Reimbursed from bank account	39
	60

Payments:

	VAT £	Net £	
Postage		11	
Travel and subsistence	3	17	
Other expenditure	2	14	
			47
Balance at 31 May 19X5			13

Your work should be neat, legible and accurate. Use the ledger working paper provided.

Tasks

(1)   Enter the credit sales and credit purchases into the appropriate ledger accounts.

(2)   Enter the bank receipts and payments from the bank current account into the other ledger accounts concerned.

(3)   Enter the petty cash payments from the petty cash summary into the other ledger accounts concerned.

(4)   Balance off all accounts in the debtors' and creditors' ledgers, and bring forward the balances at 1 June.

(5)   Balance off all the accounts in the general ledger at 31 May, except those where there are no new entries during May. Where there are entries on only one side of an account, you need only draw a single line on that side and show the new balance at 31 May, as a sub-total. Otherwise balance the accounts and bring forward the balances to 1 June.

(6)   A list of general ledger account headings is attached. Enter all balances at 1 June including the bank and petty cash balances. Total the two columns. They should agree, but leave the work incomplete if you are unable to trace the errors within the time you have allowed for the exercise.

DEBTORS' LEDGER

Willowes Ltd

Date	Details	Amount £	Date	Details	Amount £
1 May	Balance b/f	442			

Howard & Howard

Date	Details	Amount £	Date	Details	Amount £
1 May	Balance b/f	387			

Chapman Ltd

Date	Details	Amount £	Date	Details	Amount £
			1 May	Balance b/f	83

Beaumann & Baker

Date	Details	Amount £	Date	Details	Amount £
1 May	Balance b/f	320			

Other customers

Date	Details	Amount £	Date	Details	Amount £
1 May	Balance b/f	35,474			

CREDITORS' LEDGER

Atwood & Co

Date	Details	Amount £	Date	Details	Amount £
			1 May	Balance b/f	4,069

Karlin & Partners

Date	Details	Amount £	Date	Details	Amount £
			1 May	Balance b/f	3,503

Hardy Ltd

Date	Details	Amount £	Date	Details	Amount £
			1 May	Balance b/f	2,794

Other suppliers

Date	Details	Amount £	Date	Details	Amount £
			1 May	Balance b/f	9,705

GENERAL LEDGER

Sales

Date	Details	Amount £	Date	Details	Amount £
			1 May	Balance b/f	91,615

Purchases

Date	Details	Amount £	Date	Details	Amount £
1 May	Balance b/f	56,776			

Debtors' control account

Date	Details	Amount £	Date	Details	Amount £
1 May	Balance b/f	36,623	1 May	Balance b/f	83

Creditors' control account

Date	Details	Amount £	Date	Details	Amount £
			1 May	Balance b/f	20,071

VAT account

Date	Details	Amount £	Date	Details	Amount £
			1 May	Balance b/f	16,195

Discounts allowed

Date	Details	Amount £	Date	Details	Amount £
1 May	Balance b/f	297			

Discounts received

Date	Details	Amount £	Date	Details	Amount £
			1 May	Balance b/f	564

Stock

Date	Details	Amount £	Date	Details	Amount £
1 May	Balance b/f	37,415			

Wages and salaries

Date	Details	Amount £	Date	Details	Amount £
1 May	Balance b/f	20,814			

Postage and stationery

Date	Details	Amount £	Date	Details	Amount £
1 May	Balance b/f	1,247			

Travel and subsistence

Date	Details	Amount £	Date	Details	Amount £
1 May	Balance b/f	757			

Other expenditure

Date	Details	Amount £	Date	Details	Amount £
1 May	Balance b/f	3,432			

Telephones

Date	Details	Amount £	Date	Details	Amount £

Repairs and renewals

Date	Details	Amount £	Date	Details	Amount £
1 May	Balance b/f	697			

Fixed assets

Date	Details	Amount £	Date	Details	Amount £
1 May	Balance b/f	171,450			

Capital

Date	Details	Amount £	Date	Details	Amount £
			1 May	Balance b/f	233,643

General ledger balances at 31 May 19X5

	Debit £	Credit £
Sales		
Purchases		
Debtors' control account		
Creditors' control account		
VAT		
Discounts allowed		
Discounts received		
Stocks		
Wages and salaries		
Postage and stationery		
Travel and subsistence		
Other expenditure		
Telephones		
Repairs and renewals		
Fixed assets		
Capital and reserves		
Cash at bank		
Petty cash		
Totals		

Returning purchases

REVISION TOPICS

Returns of goods to suppliers may be due to faulty goods, excess goods, unauthorised goods or unsold goods purchased on a *sale or return* basis. Returns are recorded on a *returns outwards note*.

A *credit note* will be received from the supplier, checked against the returns outwards note and recorded in the *purchase returns day book*. This is analysed and posted in a similar manner to the purchase day book.

REVISION QUESTIONS

1   Dave runs a small independent petrol station, buying his petrol and oil from a number of suppliers who fax him every day to inform him of the latest prices. On 8 June he buys 10,000 litres of unleaded petrol at 40p per litre. When the invoice arrives on 18 June he discovers that he has been invoiced for 11,000 litres. On 18 June the supplier's fax indicates that the price of unleaded petrol has fallen to 38.3p per litre.

Which price per litre is applicable for the credit note for 1,000 litres of unleaded petrol which will be issued to Dave?

2   What is the document called which records returns to suppliers and how is each part of this document used?

3   An invoice is found to be incorrect and a credit note is requested. Should the invoice be processed as usual or processed only when a credit note is obtained?

4   What entry/entries would be made in respect of a credit note for purchases to the value of £100 plus VAT at 17$\frac{1}{2}$% from Janitorial Supplies Ltd

(a)   in the creditors' ledger; and
(b)   in the nominal ledger?

5   The following credit transactions occurred in September 19X1:

	£
Purchase invoices received	12,000
Purchase invoices paid	11,400
Cash purchases	2,600
Discounts received	840
Credit notes received	756

The balance on the creditors' ledger control account on 1 September 19X1 was £1,890. What is the balance on 30 September 19X1?

6 An error is made when casting the 'Total' column in a purchase returns day book which has analysis columns for total, VAT and purchase returns only. Will this error affect the

(a)	creditors ledger control account?	Yes/No
(b)	creditors ledger accounts?	Yes/No
(c)	purchases?	Yes/No

BOOKKEEPING EXERCISE

Data

The following transactions all occurred on 1 March 19X4 and have been entered for you into summarised books of original entry. VAT has been calculated to the nearest pount at a rate of 17.5% and you should continue to use this rate for any subsequent calculations.

Treat 'other customers' and 'other suppliers' as individual accounts.

Sales day book

	Total £	VAT £	Net £
Lewis & Alcott	5,393	803	4,590
Fassett & Co	6,611	985	5,626
Other customers	13,964	2,080	11,884
	25,968	3,868	22,100

Purchases day book

	Total £	VAT £	Net £	Goods for resale £	Telephone £
Prittchett Ltd	11,630	1,732	9,898	9,898	
Murdoch Bros	8,863	1,320	7,543	7,543	
English Telecomm	841	125	716		716
Selincourt & Partners	3,782	563	3,219	3,219	
Other suppliers	12,927	1,925	11,002	11,002	
	38,043	5,665	32,378	31,662	716

Purchases returns day book

	Total £	VAT £	Net £
Murdoch Bros	2,115	315	1,800
Selincourt & Partners	1,093	163	930
	3,208	478	2,730

Cash book

Opening balance at start of day   15,398 (debit)

Receipts:

	Discount £	Amount received £	
Fassett & Co	87	4,331	
		4,331	
			4,331

Payments:

	Discount £	Total amount paid £	VAT £	
Murdoch Bros	118	5,890		
Prittchett Ltd		640		
Selincourt & Partners		1,529		
Rent payable		2,500		
Bank charges		45		
Cash purchases		643	96	
Other suppliers		9,516		
				20,763

The following balances are available to you at the start of the day on 1 March 19X4.

Customers:

	£
Lewis & Alcott	11,952
Fassett & Co	4,418
Other customers	480,691

Suppliers:

	£
Prittchett Ltd	23,820
Murdoch Bros	8,123
Selincourt & Partners	6,543
English Telecomm	–
Other suppliers	267,339

Other:

	£
Purchases	2,543,560
Sales	4,173,893
Sales returns	11,084
Purchases returns	10,926
Telephone	–
Rent payable	5,000
Bank charges	91
VAT (credit balance)	72,108
Discount allowed	20,319
Discount received	9,627
Debtors' control account	497,061
Creditors' control account	305,825
Various other debit balances – total	2,002,119
Various other credit balances – total	522,253

Complete all the following tasks

Tasks

(1)   Enter the opening balances into the following accounts:

Debtors' control account
Creditors' control account
Telephone
Purchases
VAT
Pritchett Ltd
Murdoch Bros
Selincourt & Partners

Use the working papers provided.

(2)   Enter all relevant entries into the accounts shown in task (1).

(3)   Balance off all the accounts in which you have made entries in task (2).

(4)   Calculate the closing balances of the remaining accounts.

Extract the list of creditors ledger balances and reconcile them to the balance on the creditors control account.

(5)   Complete the list of balances by inserting the updated figure for each account in either the debit balances column or the credit balances column as appropriate. Total the two columns.

The two totals should be the same. If they do not agree, try to trace and correct any errors you have made within the time you have available. If you are still unable to make the totals balance, leave the work incomplete.

Note: It is not a requirement to draw up all the individual accounts in order to calculate the closing balances for task (5). Candidates may, however, adopt that approach if they wish.

GENERAL LEDGER

Debtors' control account

Date	Details	Amount £	Date	Details	Amount £

Creditors' control account

Date	Details	Amount £	Date	Details	Amount £

Telephone

Date	Details	Amount £	Date	Details	Amount £

Purchases

Date	Details	Amount £	Date	Details	Amount £

VAT

Date	Details	Amount £	Date	Details	Amount £

CREDITORS' LEDGER

Pritchett Ltd

Date	Details	Amount £	Date	Details	Amount £

Murdoch Bros

Date	Details	Amount £	Date	Details	Amount £

Selincourt & Partners

Date	Details	Amount £	Date	Details	Amount £

List of updated balances at the end of the day

	Debit £	Credit £
Suppliers		
Prittchett Ltd		
Murdoch Bros		
Selincourt & Partners		
English Telecomm		
Other suppliers		
Total		
Creditors control account		
Purchases		
Sales		
Sales returns		
Purchases returns		
Debtors' control account		
Creditors' control account		
Telephone		
Rent payable		
Bank charges		
VAT		
Bank		
Discount allowed		
Discount received		
Other debit balances	2,002,119	
Other credit balances		522,253
Total		

Using information about creditors

REVISION TOPICS

A *suppliers' statement reconciliation* is a form of internal control. It compares the *suppliers' statements* with the individual creditors accounts in the creditors' ledger. Errors detected in this way will have to be corrected in the creditors' ledger and/or the creditors' ledger control account. Sometimes differences between a statement and the creditors' ledger control account are due to timing differences; these are not adjusted for as they reverse in a subsequent period.

REVISION QUESTIONS

1   On a suppliers' statement reconciliation, which of the items below should be deducted from the balance per suppliers' statement?

     (a)   Cash in transit
     (b)   Goods in transit

2   During the reconciliation of suppliers' statements, Marianne discovers that invoice 272 from IC Frozen Foods Ltd has been recorded in the creditors ledger as £852 instead of £258. She traces the error back to the initial recording of the invoice in the purchase day book total column. What amendments will need to be made in the ledgers to adjust for this error?

3   Examine the supplier's statement and creditors ledger account in respect of Drill-it Machine Tools Ltd below:

```
                    DRILL-IT MACHINE TOOLS LTD
                         24 SURREY STREET
                        BEDFORD MK20 8PJ


              Statement of account              30 April 19X0


    Small Tool Hire Co
    3 Bramall Road
    Northampton
    NO1 2FR
```

Date	Transaction	Total £
1.4.X4	Balance brought forward	2,041.18
2.4.X4	Invoice 813	608.99
8.4.X4	Invoice 828	1,477.80
10.4.X4	Received with thanks	(1,082.90)
13.4.X4	Credit note 61	(85.10)
20.4.X4	Invoice 856	200.03
28.4.X4	Invoice 864	126.20
	Balance due at 30 April 19X4	3,286.20

Creditors ledger
Drill-It Machine Tools Ltd   **(21)**

Date	Transaction	£	Date	Transaction	£
17.4.X4	Credit note X44	85.10	1.4.X4	Balance b/f	958.28
30.4.X4	Cheque 000963	873.18	5.4.X4	Invoice D144	608.99
			10.4.X4	Invoice D151	1,477.80
			25.4.X4	Invoice D172	200.03
30.4.X4	Balance c/f	2,286.82			
		3,245.10			3,245.10

What adjustments are required in the ledgers in respect of any discrepancies you find?

4   Which two documents sent by the supplier to the customer often feature a detachable remittance advice?

5   With the agreement of Smallfry Ltd a contra entry has been made in the debtors and creditors ledger accounts for Smallfry Ltd, but not in the nominal ledger. Would this error be discovered by performing:

    (a)   a suppliers' statement reconciliation?   Yes/No

    (b)   a creditors' ledger reconciliation?   Yes/No

    (c)   a trial balance?   Yes/No

6   You are the creditors ledger clerk at Astro-Models Ltd. Whilst performing a suppliers' statement reconciliation for Aeropics Ltd, a new customer, you notice that they have deducted payments in respect of invoice numbers 00851 and 00863, but have not deducted the 2% settlement discounts of £40 and £63 respectively; you can tell from the statements that the payments were received within the time limits for the discounts.

Write a letter to Aeropics Ltd requesting that the discount be honoured.

Mock central assessment

FOUNDATION STAGE: FINANCIAL ACCOUNTING (UNITS 1 AND 2)

Time allowed – 3 hours

This assessment is in three parts.

PART 1

Processing exercise

Complete all tasks.

PART 2

20 Short answer questions

Complete all questions.

PART 3

Communicating accounting information

Complete all three tasks.

The tasks and questions are all based on the transactions of Hotel and Domestic Ltd. This company buys a range of catering equipment and cooking utensils and sells it to the catering trade on credit terms. It operates from a warehouse in Doncaster and from a recently opened showroom, with an office above, across the road from the warehouse. The showroom also sells small items direct to the public on cash terms only.

The Managing Director is Phil Walker and Susan Field is the Accountant. You are the Accounting Technician, reporting to Susan Field.

Data

The following extracts from the books of prime entry show the transactions of Hotel and Domestic Ltd on Tuesday 7 January 19X8.

VAT has been calculated to the nearest £. Treat 'other customers' and 'other suppliers' as individual accounts.

Sales day book

	Total £	*VAT* £	*Net* £
Manor Hotels Ltd	2,005	299	1,706
Bistro Renee	530	79	451
Ridings College	6,223	927	5,296
Dunrovan Rest Home	2,915	434	2,481
Other customers	1,743	260	1,483
	13,416	1,999	11,417

Purchase day book

	Total £	*VAT* £	*Goods for resale* £	*Rent* £	*Entertaining* £
Vic's Mixers	6,452	961	5,491		
Brisk Whisks Ltd	335	50	285		
Johnson & Co	800			800	
Manor Hotels Ltd	573				573
Other suppliers	2,348	350	1,998		
	10,508	1,361	7,774	800	573

Purchase returns day book

	Total £	*VAT* £	*Goods for resale* £
Vic's Mixers	428	64	364

Journal

	Debit £	*Credit* £
Bad debts	270	
Debtors control account		270

The Peacock Tearooms balance written-off

	Debit £	*Credit* £
Discounts allowed	48	
Bad debts		48

Correction of an error made on 3 January 19X8

Cash book

	Cheque No.	Total £	VAT £	Net £	Discount £
Receipts:					
Ridings College		1,840	–	1,840	38
Cash sales		381	57	324	
		2,221	57	2,164	38
Payments:					
Vic's Mixers	001797	2,450	–	2,450	50

Balance at start of day	295 (overdrawn)
Balance at end of day	524 (overdrawn)

The following are *selected balances only* at the start of the day on 7 January 19X8.

Customers

	£
Manor Hotels Ltd	4,612
Ridings College	1,878
Peacock Tearooms	270
Other customers	16,125

Suppliers

	£
Vic's Mixers	4,060
Manor Hotels Ltd	Nil
Brisk Whisks Ltd	899
Johnson & Co	800
Other suppliers	15,929

Other

Sales	1,362,176
Purchases	810,430
Sales returns	8,812
Purchases returns	2,672
VAT	24,349 (credit balance)
Debtors control account	22,885
Creditors control account	21,688
Rent	4,800
Discounts received	14,962
Discounts allowed	12,115
Entertaining	1,870
Bad debts	128
Bank	295
Other debit balances	1,003,798
Other credit balances	438,696

PART 1 – PROCESSING EXERCISE

Task 1   Enter the opening balances into the following accounts:

- Debtors' control account

- Creditors' control account

- Purchases

- VAT

- Rent

- Ridings College

- Vic's Mixers

These accounts may be found on the following pages.

Task 2   Enter all relevant transactions into the accounts shown in Task 1.

Task 3   Balance off all the accounts in which you have made entries in Task 2.

Task 4   Calculate the closing balances of the remaining supplier accounts and complete the list of balances.

Task 5   Reconcile the closing balance of the creditors control account to the total of the list of closing supplier balances prepared in Task 4.

Task 6   Calculate the closing balances of the remaining general ledger accounts and complete the list of balances.

The two column totals should be the same. If they do not agree try to trace and correct any errors you have made within the time available. If you are still unable to make the totals balance, leave the work incomplete.

Notes

(1)   It is not a requirement to draw up all the individual accounts in order to calculate the closing balances for tasks 4 and 6. Candidates may, however, adopt that approach if they wish.

(2)   Blank working sheets will be provided in the real Central Assessment.

GENERAL LEDGER

Debtors' control account

Date	Details	Amount £	Date	Details	Amount £

Creditors' control account

Date	Details	Amount £	Date	Details	Amount £

Purchases

Date	Details	Amount £	Date	Details	Amount £

Rent

Date	Details	Amount £	Date	Details	Amount £

VAT

Date	Details	Amount £	Date	Details	Amount £

DEBTORS' LEDGER

Ridings College

Date	Details	Amount £	Date	Details	Amount £

CREDITORS' LEDGER

Vic's Mixers

Date	Details	Amount £	Date	Details	Amount £

	£	£
Updated creditors control account		....

Updated supplier balances

	£
Vic's Mixers	....
Manor Hotels Ltd	....
Brisk Whisks Ltd	....
Johnson & Co	....
Other suppliers	....
Total updated supplier balances	....

List of updated general ledger balances at the end of the day:

	Debit balances £	*Credit balances* £
Sales	....	....
Sales returns	....	....
Purchases	....	....
Purchases returns	....	....
Rent	....	....
Entertaining	....	....
Bad debts	....	....
Debtors control account	....	....
Creditors control account	....	....
VAT	....	....
Bank	....	....
Discount allowed	....	....
Discount received	....	....
Other debit balances	1,003,798	....
Other credit balances	....	438,696
Totals		

PART 2 – SHORT ANSWER QUESTIONS

Using where appropriate the information given in Part 1, write in the space provided or circle the correct answer.

1 On 9 January a bank statement was received dated 7 January. During the preparation of the bank reconciliation statement, you discover unpresented cheques of £2,450 and deposits in transit of £2,221. The balance per bank statement of £2,864 will be

    (a)   reduced by £229
    (b)   increased by £229

2 The following items are found on the bank statement but do not appear in the cash book. In each case, state the double entry which would need to be performed in the general ledger to adjust for that item.

    (a)   A customer's cheque for £2,646 dishonoured by their bank

        Debit .... £ .... Credit .... £ ....

    (b)   Standing order for insurance of £430

        Debit .... £ .... Credit .... £ ....

    (c)   Bank charges of £83

        Debit .... £ .... Credit .... £ ....

3 Suggest four reasons why the customer's bank would not honour their cheque, given that the cheque is physically intact and not endorsed in any way.

    ....

    ....

    ....

    ....

4 When a bank makes a payment by standing order on behalf of a customer, what legal relationships exist between the bank and the customer?

    Bank ....   Customer ....

5   Hotel and Domestic Ltd bank cheques and cash takings daily, making use of the nightsafe at the Town Street branch of the Four Counties Bank. Explain briefly the advantages of using this service at regular intervals.

....

....

....

....

6   A customer sends a purchase order to Hotel and Domestic Ltd by fax on 7 January. Having received the 19X8 price list from Hotel and Domestic Ltd on 4 January, the order is placed for 200 dinner plates (white) at £3.40 each including VAT. Hotel and Domestic post their sales order confirmation to the customer on 8 January and it is received by them on 9 January. A valid contract now exists between Hotel and Domestic Ltd and the customer, comprising an offer, acceptance and consideration to be provided by both parties.

   (a)   On what date was the offer made?

          ....

   (b)   On what date was the offer accepted?

          ....

   (c)   What consideration is to be provided by Hotel and Domestic Ltd?

          ....

   (d)   What consideration is to be provided by the customer?

          ....

7   It is the policy of the company to issue a refund for faulty goods to a retail customer only if the customer can produce a receipt.

   (a)   Is this policy in accordance with the law?

          ....

   (b)   Explain your answer briefly.

          ....

          ....

8 The company offers a settlement discount of 2¹/₂% to customers who pay within 30 days of the invoice date. An invoice is sent to a customer on 8 January for an oven, the listed selling price of which is £8,200 (excluding VAT of 17.5%).

(a) If the customer pays within 30 days, how much will he pay?

....

(b) How will this transaction be recorded in the VAT control account?

As a *debit/credit* entry for £ ....

9 A regular customer, Jonah's Steakhouses, has returned some faulty sets of cutlery. The returned goods are received at the warehouse where a document is raised to record their return.

(a) What document is used to record the goods returned as they are received in the warehouse?

....

(b) Explain how this document can help to exercise internal control over credit notes.

....

....

....

....

10 A credit note is issued to Jonah's Steakhouses in respect of the faulty goods.

(a) List six pieces of information which should appear on the credit note of a VAT registered business.

....

....

....

....

....

....

(b) State which account will be debited and which account will be credited in respect of the credit note in the general ledger. (Ignore the effect of VAT.)

Debit .... Credit ....

(c)   Will any further adjustment of the ledgers be required in respect of this transaction?

....

Explain your answer.

....

....

11   Hotel and Domestic Ltd makes sundry cash purchases from the petty cash imprest of £100. Each Monday a cheque is cashed at the bank to replenish the imprest. During the week ending 10 January 19X8, vouchers supporting petty cash payments totalled £93. How much cash will be drawn from the business bank account on Monday 13 January?

....

12   Purchase invoices received from suppliers are authorised by Phil Walker before entering their details in the purchase day book. What checks could he perform to authorise an invoice for a quarterly gas bill?

....

....

....

....

....

....

13   Each month a statement of account is received from the suppliers. You are currently checking the statements covering purchases up to 31 December 19X7 by comparing them with supplier's accounts in the creditors ledger. You discover two errors in the creditors ledger.

(a)   A credit note for £87 from Hot Plates plc has been credited to the account of Handy Oven Mitts Ltd.

(b)   An invoice from Briteburn Ovens plc for goods for resale of £7,980 has been recorded as £7,890 in their account.

Explain briefly how these errors would be corrected in the creditors ledger.

(a)   ....

....

....

(b) ....

....

....

14 The error in 13 (b) above was traced back to the initial recording of the Briteburn Oven's plc invoice in the purchase day book.

What double entry in the general ledger is required, if any.

Debit ....£ ....   Credit ....£ ....

or

No adjustment required in the general ledger.

15 Explain briefly how a monthly reconciliation of the debtors control account and a list of individual debtors balances can be helpful to a business.

....

....

....

....

16 Which of the following errors would require adjustment to the debtors control account?

(a) Discount allowed not recorded in the cash book   Yes/No

(b) Casting error in the 'total' column of the sales returns day book   Yes/No

(c) Casting error in the 'total' column of the cash book   Yes/No

(d) Omission of a debtor's balance from the list of balances   Yes/No

17 The account of Al's Drive-In contains the following entries:

			£
October 17	Invoice	763	233
November 20	Invoice	792	115
December 5	Invoice	811	97
December 12	Invoice	817	48
December 20	Cheque	P317	(228)
December 20	Discount	CB12	(5)

Produce an age analysis as at 31 December 19X7 for this customer by completing the following table:

Total £	Current £	30+ days £	60+ days £

18 The offices above the new showroom are not yet fully furbished and various items of expenditure are incurred in January in respect of the offices. Categorise each of the following items as either capital or revenue expenditure:

(a)	Two word processors	Capital/Revenue
(b)	Software for the word processors	Capital/Revenue
(c)	Stationery for the word processors	Capital/Revenue
(d)	Maintenance contract for the word processors	Capital/Revenue

19 At present, the employees at Hotel and Domestic Ltd are paid monthly by cheque. Give two further methods of making these monthly salary payments, other than payment in cash.

....

....

20 John French would like to buy goods on credit from Hotel and Domestic Ltd on a regular basis. He says that his bank will confirm his credit worthiness and gives written permission for this. Will Hotel and Domestic be able to obtain details of John French's bank account from his bank?

....

Explain your answer.

....

....

....

....

PART 3 – COMMUNICATING ACCOUNTING INFORMATION

Task 1

Manor Hotels Ltd is a regular customer. In December, however, they supplied a buffet lunch at the formal opening of the new showroom and consequently appear in the creditors ledger also. Susan Field has asked you to write a letter to the credit controller at Manor Hotels Ltd requesting that a contra be performed in respect of their debtors ledger and creditors ledger balance of £6,617 and £573 respectively.

Using the headed paper on the following page, draft a suitable letter to be sent to the credit controller of Manor Hotels Ltd.

Task 1

$\mathcal{H}$ & $\mathcal{D}$

Hotel & Domestic Ltd
143 Park Road
Doncaster DN3 2YY

Task 2

Phil Walker has considered the introduction of payment by credit card facilities in the showroom; at present, only cash and cheques supported by guarantee cards are accepted. He is sceptical that customers will increase as a result because they can all pay by cheque in any case and he is reluctant to pay commission to the credit card companies. He has asked you to assess the situation.

Write a memorandum to Phil Walker on the internal documentation provided, stating briefly the advantages to the customer and the business of offering the facility to pay by credit card.

Task 2

H & D

MEMORANDUM

To: **Date:**

From:

Task 3

A purchase order has been received from the Moss Park Hotel for goods totalling £2,496 including VAT. You notice that their current balance in the debtors ledger is £3,970 and that their credit limit, as set by Phil Walker, is £5,000. Closer scrutiny of their account reveals that this amount has been outstanding for four months and that a previous communication with this customer did not reveal any problems with the goods delivered or invoice sent. Phil Walker decides that their credit limit should not be increased and that they may only be supplied with further goods when they have cleared their existing balance.

Write a suitable letter to John Rogers, the proprietor of the Moss Park Hotel.

Task 3

H & D

**Hotel & Domestic Ltd
143 Park Road
Doncaster DN3 2YY**

93

Task 3

Answers to revision questions

SESSION 1

1   Convenient use of coins and notes.

   (a)   To pay for small amounts such as newspapers, milk and window-cleaning
   (b)   To give change in cash transactions
   (c)   To pay wages to employees who do not have bank accounts (now rare)

2   Which are true?

   (a)   (i), (ii), (iii) and (iv)

   Some current accounts do earn interest, but at rates much lower than those of deposit accounts.

   (b)   (i), (ii) and (v)

   Some deposit accounts allow the use of cheque books.

3   (b)   These cheques will not appear individually; they will appear only as part of the totals paid in each Thursday.

4   The safest way of sending money through the post, if you have not got a bank account, is by means of a postal order. A £5 postal order can be bought from a Post Office and stamps to the value of 15p will be added to top up its value to £5.15. The name of the mail order firm to be paid is written on the postal order and it can then be sent through the post.

5   The details to be filled in by the account-holder are as follows:

   •   date

   •   payee

   •   amount in words

   •   amount in numbers

   •   signature

6   (a)   This cannot be used as legal tender as the limit for 10p pieces of £5 is exceeded.

   (b)   This may be used as the 20p limit for 1p pieces has not been exceeded and £1 coins are unlimited legal tender.

SESSION 2

1

		£
£81.48	Invoice amount	84.00
	Discount 3% × 84	2.52
	Cash received 97% × 84	81.48

2

		£
£253	Invoice amount $\dfrac{100}{98}$ × 247.94	253.00
	Discount $\dfrac{2}{98}$ × 247.94	5.06
	Cash received 98%	247.94

3

Customer	Invoice number	£	Discount allowed
Beth Brown	2714	107.25	2.75

4   Six from:

Discount incorrectly calculated
Discount taken outside the time limit
Payment disagrees with remittance advice
Incorrectly signed cheque
Payee incorrect on cheque
Amount on cheque incorrect
Words and figures on cheque disagree

5   Errors and omissions excepted. It indicates that the seller is claiming the right to correct any genuine errors on the invoice at a later date.

6

AN Other
2 High Street
Wakefield
West Yorkshire
WK1 3JV

Ben Battersby
3 Potters Lane
Barnsley
South Yorkshire
S35 6AU

22 January 1994

Dear Mr Battersby

Remittance in respect of invoice H483

Thank you for your prompt remittance in respect of invoice H483. Unfortunately, the date on the cheque is incorrectly recorded as 1993 rather than 1994 and we are therefore unable to accept it in payment of the invoice in its present form.

I therefore enclose the cheque and would be grateful if it could be corrected and returned to me, or a replacement cheque issued.

I look forward to hearing from you.

Yours sincerely

AN Other

SESSION 3

1   Eight from:

- name of supplier

- address of supplier

- VAT registration number of supplier

- invoice number

- date of sale

- name of customer

- address of customer

- nature of transaction (eg. sale)

- description and quantity of goods or services

- for each item

    – VAT rate
    – amount excluding VAT (in sterling)

- total amount excluding VAT (in sterling)

- amount of VAT chargeable at each rate

- total VAT payable

- amount payable including VAT (in sterling)

2   £

Amount excluding VAT (10 × £36)   360.00
VAT (17^1/$_2$% × £360)   63.00
                                                                    ———
Payable to Fyne Wynes Ltd   423.00
                                                                    ———

3   £

(a)   Discounted amount excluding VAT (6 × £250 × 98%)   1,470.00
       Discounted VAT (17^1/$_2$% × 1,470)   257.25
                                                                   ————
       Payable to Myers Tyres Ltd   1,727.25
                                                                   ————

			£
(b)	Amount excluding VAT (6 × £250)		1,500.00
	Discounted VAT (17$^1/_2$% × 1,500 × 98%)		257.25
	Payable to Myers Tyres Ltd		1,757.25

4 Payments to

	£
Ambrose Ltd (431.24 – 10.78 + 73.58)	494.04
Artgraphic (29.50 + 5.01)	34.51
Andy's Autos (605.73 – 15.14 + 103.35)	693.94
Total payments	1,222.49

5 Unused cheques are controlled by locking them away in a safe which may be accessed only by a limited number of authorised personnel.

6 No, these should not be destroyed. They should be cancelled on their face so that they cannot be used and kept in the safe. This ensures that all cheques can be accounted for.

SESSION 4

1 Yes. The details on the receipt are sufficient to qualify as a VAT receipt for a retailer.

2 (b) A cheque for £50 and £14 cash is the only payment which would be guaranteed. (a) exceeds the £50 limit and (c) involves two cheques for the same transaction.

3 (a) Yes
(b) Yes
(c) No
(d) Yes

4 (b)

5 Yes. The retailer still has to check that the signature on the sales voucher corresponds with the signature on the credit card.

6

Ron's Records
53 Bayview Road
Exmouth
Devon EX14 2PT

5 May 19X4

Mr C Crabbe
2 Ropers Avenue
Exmouth
Devon EX17 4SU

Dear Mr Crabbe

Refunds under the Sales of Goods Act

Thank you for your letter regarding your recent purchases from us and I apologise for any inconvenience that has been caused by the various problems you have experienced. You are correct in pointing out that you do not need a receipt to claim a refund and I shall indeed make refunds for all items qualifying under the Sale of Goods Act as detailed below.

Under the Act, your cracked CD requires a refund as it is clearly faulty. Similarly the CD which had the wrong case requires a refund as the item you bought was not as described. Also, the Act requires refunds for items which are unsuitable for the purpose specified by the customer, as is the case with the tape cassette which was unsuitable for your daughter's party. However, I am unable to give you a refund for the other tape cassette as we had no agreement that you could change your mind about this purchase. Nevertheless, it is my policy to offer a credit note in such instances as a gesture of goodwill.

If you return the purchases to the shop, I will be pleased to issue you with a refund and a credit note for the appropriate amounts. I hope this meets with your satisfaction.

Your sincerely

Ron Smith
Proprietor
Ron's Records

SESSION 5

1   The cheque will be sent by the Church Lane, Worcester branch to Lloyds bank's clearing department and then on to the Parliament Street branch. The Central Clearing House is not involved as there is only one clearing bank.

2   A general endorsement is the payee's signature on the back of a cheque. This makes the cheque payable to the bearer. It enables a cheque to be transferred from the payee to a third party without banking it and writing out a new cheque with the third party as payee.

3   (a)   No
     (b)   Yes
     (c)   No

4   Pamela Poppins may pay the cheque into her sole account as long as it has been endorsed by Mr J Poppins.

5 The main advantage to the employee of being paid through BACS rather than by bank giro credit is that money is transferred immediately into their account – they do not have to wait for the payment to clear through the credit clearing system.

6 This cheque would not be valid for two reasons. Firstly it is not to a named person or the bearer and secondly it is conditional on the amount of money in the account.

SESSION 6

1

	Date	Narrative	Cheque No.	Total £	VAT £	Creditors £	Purchases £
(a)	6 July	Cash purchases		53 (45×1.175)	8		45
(b)		Frank Field		98 (83×1.175)		98	
(c)		Cash purchases		27	4 $(27 \times \dfrac{17.5}{117.5})$		23

2 A folio is a reference showing the destination of a posting. In a cash book which is part of the double-entry system, it would give the ledger to which the individual transactions are posted.

3 Dr Creditors ledger control £3.35
   Cr Discounts received £3.35

4

	£	
Total	172.73	$(150 \times 98\% \times 117.5\%)$
Cash sales	147.00	$(150 \times 98\%)$
Debtors	0.00	
VAT	25.73	$(147 \times 17.5\%)$
Discounts allowed	3.00	$(150 \times 2\%)$

5

	£
Balance per bank statement	279.04
Add: Deposits in transit	23.50
Less: Unpresented cheques	(8.43)
Balance per cash book	294.11

The balance in the cash book is £294.11 on 30 September 1994.

6   Memorandum

To:	Freda Frith, Trainee Accounting Technician
From:	Susan Sparks, Accounting Technician
Date:	18 November 1994
Subject:	Standing orders in bank reconciliations

I notice from your bank reconciliation that you have included a standing order as a reconciling item. Reconciling items normally represents payments or receipts of the business which, due to the time lag between the business' transaction and its recording by the bank, have not yet appeared on the bank statement. Thus, our bank reconciliation effectively brings the bank statement up to date.

A standing order, however, is different as this is a payment that the business has authorised to make on its behalf and therefore the bank is up to date, but the business is not. In this case, we must update the business by including the standing order in the cash book and finding the adjusted cash book total.

SESSION 7

1   (a)   Yes
       (b)   No
       (c)   Yes

2   The bank is the bailee.

3   The bank is responsible for ensuring that there are no mistakes on a bank account.

4   A lien is the right to keep goods as payment for a debt. A bank has the right to exercise a lien over the customer's property in the bank's possession such as cheques paid in by the customer, but not valuables in safe deposit boxes.

5   Five from:

- to pay customer's cheques

- to obey any express mandate

- to keep customer's details confidential

- to give reasonable notice of closure of accounts

- to provide regular bank statements

- to tell customers their account balance when asked

- to accept cash and cheques paid in by customers

- to repay customer's money when the customer asks

- to tell customers immediately of any possible forgery

- to exercise proper skill and care

6   The bank was acting within its rights when they charged Thomas Timms for their services when he went overdrawn. It is common for banks to exercise their right to make a charge only when the customer is overdrawn. The bank will have credited his account as a goodwill gesture rather than because it was not entitled to make the charges.

SESSION 8

1   £

Petty cash   75
Vouchers and related receipts   25
                                                                                               ——
Pre-set level   100
                                                                                               ——

∴ The cash in the cash box is £75.

2   Five from:

- sequential number

- authorisation signature

- signature of recipient of petty cash payment

- date

- description of item purchased

- amount

- general ledger code

3   £   £

Dr: Postage   23
       Cleaning   18
       Refreshments   52
       Newspapers   12
       VAT   12

Cr: Petty cash   117

4   (a)   Wages would not be paid through petty cash as there is official documentation to be completed.

5   Dr: Petty cash   Cr: Bank

6

P Parkin
12 Fish Street
Beverley
Hull
HU18 3PD

D Dawson
Unit 5
Station Industrial Park
Hull
HU3 3QR

14 May 1994

Dear Daniel

Petty cash imprest system

I am glad to hear that your business is thriving and hope that I can improve your efficiency by suggesting a way for you to control petty cash payments.

Setting up the system

An imprest system replenishes a petty cash float up to the same level at the start of each week; £100 would probably be an appropriate amount for the cash requirements of your business. To begin with, cash a business cheque at the bank for £100 and keep this amount in a petty cash box. Each time a payment is made, complete a petty cash voucher giving details of the payment and attach the receipt to the voucher. Keep the completed vouchers in the petty cash box. At the start of the next week, the vouchers will add up to the amount spent in the previous week and a cheque can be cashed for that amount to replenish the petty cash. The completed vouchers will be filed.

Recording the payments

A petty cash book could be maintained detailing the cash payments and cheques cashed to top up the float. A sequential number for each voucher could also be recorded in the petty cash book to ensure that payments are not 'lost'.

Security over petty cash

The petty cash box should be locked in the safe at all times. Similar control should also be exercised over petty cash vouchers.

Do not hesitate to contact me should you require any further information.

Yours sincerely

P Parkin

SESSION 9

1   The copies could be used as follows:

    (a)   kept by the customer for their records;
    (b)   kept by the despatch department;
    (c)   sent to the stores to update stock records;
    (d)   sent to the sales invoicing department to raise an invoice.

2   Control totals are being used here.

3

	£
1,750 @ £1	1,750.00
Less: Discount @ 2$1/2$%	(43.75)
	1,706.25
Add: VAT @ 17$1/2$%	298.59
	2,004.84

The invoice total will be £2,004.84.

4   The date of supply of the goods is called the *basic tax point*. If the invoice is made out after the date of supply, the date is called the *actual tax point*.

5   This indicates to the customer that the invoice price excludes delivery to his or her premises and that the customer must therefore organise and pay for delivery of the goods.

6   A customer is put on a stop list when it is considered too risky to supply them with more goods or services, for example if they have reached their credit limit. No more goods or services are provided until they have reduced or paid their existing debts.

SESSION 10

1   (c)   The sales day book is a book of prime entry.

2

		£	£
Dr:	Debtors' ledger control account	822.50	
	Cr: Sales		700.00
	Cr: VAT		122.50

3   **To:**   Janice Oswald, Managing Director
        From: Otto Jeeves, Accountant
        Subject: Improvements to credit sales postings

        Date: 18 April 1994

To improve the accuracy of credit sales recording I can suggest two steps which we can implement immediately.

(a)   The journal voucher should be checked and authorised by myself. Prior to posting by Oliver Johnson, I shall check to ensure:

- correct coding for accounts

- correct arithmetic

- correct debit or credit allocation; and

- correct translation from sales day book to journal voucher

(b)   Jonathan Owen should be given a period of staff training to ensure that he understands the method of completing the journal vouchers and his progress over the ensuing weeks monitored closely.

4   The sales department might set credit limits high in order to boost sales at the risk of credit control.

5   Sales invoices are used to prepare the sales day book.

6   (a)   Yes
        (b)   No
        (c)   Yes
        (d)   No

7   (a)   File
        (b)   Field
        (c)   Record

8   Any two of the following:

- Error detection is easier compared with real-time processing (use of control totals)
- Inexpensive (no special hardware or software is needed)
- Large scale economies due to bulk processing
- Flexible (part of the data can be processed now, the remainder later)
- Easy to schedule processing at set times
- Easy to control input and processing

SESSION 11

1   In the debtors' ledger a cash receipt is recorded on the credit side, reducing the amount owed by a debtor.

2   The remittance advice is usually used to match cash receipts and invoices.

3   Contra

4   £   £

(a)   Dr: Discounts allowed   20
               Cr: Debtors' ledger control account   20

       Dr: Discounts received   20
               Cr: Creditors' ledger control account   20

(b)   Wanda Wrights account requires a credit entry of £20 to record the discount allowed to her.

5   (a)   No – this only affects the totals posted to the nominal ledger.
         (b)   Yes
         (c)   No – this will affect the creditors' ledger.
         (d)   Yes

6

Debtors' ledger control account

	£		£
Balance b/f	3,750	Cash	13,004
Invoices issued	12,632	Bad debts	1,200
		Balance c/f	2,178
	16,382		16,382

The balance on debtors ledger control account on 31 October is £2,178.

Bookkeeping exercise

GENERAL LEDGER

Debtors' control account

Date	Details	Amount £	Date	Details	Amount £
1/3/X4	Balance b/f	790,614	1/3/X4	Bad debts	222
	Sales day book	65,422		Creditors control account	873
				Cash received	11,844
				Discount allowed	240
				Balance c/f	842,857
		856,036			856,036
2/3/X4	Balance b/f	842,857			

Sales

Date	Details	Amount £	Date	Details	Amount £
1/3/X4	Balance c/f	2,259,300	1/3/X4	Balance b/f	2,203,622
				Sales day book	55,678
		2,259,300			2,259,300
			2/3/X4	Balance c/f	2,259,300

VAT

Date	Details	Amount £	Date	Details	Amount £
1/3/X4	Balance c/f	45,627	1/3/X4	Balance b/f	35,883
				Sales day book	9,744
		45,627			45,627
			2/3/X4	Balance c/f	45,627

DEBTORS' LEDGER

Edward Prior & Co

Date	Details	Amount £	Date	Details	Amount £
1/3/X4	Balance b/f	8,763	1/3/X4	Cash received	4,539
	Sales day book	2,356		Discount allowed	92
				Balance c/f	6,488
		11,119			11,119
2/3/X4	Balance b/f	6,488			

Chetwynd Bros

Date	Details	Amount £	Date	Details	Amount £
1/3/X4	Balance b/f	6,036	1/3/X4	Creditors' control account	873
	Sales day book	5,578		Cash received	3,254
				Discount allowed	66
				Balance c/f	7,421
		11,614			11,614
2/3/X4	Balance b/f	7,421			

Robertson Productions Ltd

Date	Details	Amount £	Date	Details	Amount £
1/3/X4	Balance b/f	20,243	1/3/X4	Cash received	4,051
	Sales day book	11,257		Discount allowed	82
				Balance c/f	27,367
		31,500			31,500
2/3/X4	Balance b/f	27,367			

	£	£
Updated debtors' control account balances		842,857

Updated customer balances

	£
Allardyce & Sons (9,143 + 3,419)	12,562
Edward Prior & Co	6,488
Chetwynd Bros	7,421
Rothman Stores (10,475 + 1,633)	12,108
Bluntishall Supplies Ltd (29,669 + 13,769)	43,438
Robertson Productions Ltd	27,367
Yew Tree Merchants Ltd	957
Thomas Allfarthing & Co (278,351 + 2,917)	281,268
Drewitt & Sons (685 + 109)	794
Peartree Manufacturing (4,335 + 266)	4,601
Bradley Bros (18,286 + 6,838)	25,124
Other customers (404,628 + 16,323 – 222)	420,729

	£
Total updated customer balances	842,857

SESSION 12

1 (a) Yes
   (b) Yes
   (c) No
   (d) Yes

2 Four from:

- a customer has returned faulty/damaged items

- a customer has returned perfect goods with the agreement of the supplier

- a customer has returned goods not sold where a sale or return agreement exists

- to refund a customer for goods not delivered

- to settle a dispute with a customer

3   (a)   No – it should, however, be given if possible.

       (b)   Yes

       (c)   Yes

       (d)   Yes

       (e)   No

       (f)   Yes

4   The sales returns day book is used to prepare the journal entry to record credit notes in the nominal ledger.

5   (a)   Gleam Cleaners' account should be credited with £480.

       (b)   Dr   Bright Lights Ltd   £84

                Cr   Cool Shades & Co   £84

6   **To:**   Mr Moss, Financial Director

       From: Mary Mangle

       Date: 3 November 1994

The current procedure for authorisation of credit notes performs the important task of agreeing details of the credit note with the returns inwards. However, this only confirms the quantity and description of the goods and the customer returning them. I propose that we implement the following additional checks:

(a)   The original invoice should be checked to ensure that the customer has been invoiced and to obtain the price to be credited. The price list should not be relied upon to give the appropriate price as revision of prices may have occurred since invoicing the goods.

(b)   The credit note itself should be reviewed for arithmetical accuracy, correct computation of VAT, correct coding and its sequential number should follow on from the previous invoice.

These additional checks will help to ensure that we keep tight control over credits to customer's accounts.

Bookkeeping exercise

GENERAL LEDGER

Debtors' control account

Date	Details	Amount £	Date	Details	Amount £
1/4/X5	Balance b/f	480,866	1/4/X5	Sales returns	4,121
	Sales day book	96,367		Cash received	15,497
				Discount allowed	311
				Balance c/f	557,304
		577,233			577,233
2/4/X5	Balance b/f	557,304			

Office expenses

Date	Details	Amount £	Date	Details	Amount £
1/4/X5	Balance b/f	8,595	1/4/X5	Balance c/f	9,611
	Journal	31			
	Cash paid	945			
	Petty cash (47 × $^{100}/_{117.5}$)	40			
		9,611			9,611
2/4/X5	Balance b/f	9,611			

Sales

Date	Details	Amount £	Date	Details	Amount £
1/4/X5	Balance b/f	3,196,319	1/4/X5	Balance b/f	3,114,304
				Sales day book	82,015
		3,196,319			3,196,319
			2/4/X5	Balance b/f	3,196,319

VAT

Date	Details	Amount £	Date	Details	Amount £
1/4/X5	Sales returns	614	1/4/X5	Balance b/f	33,732
	Cash purchases			Sales day book	14,352
	(800 × $^{17.5}/_{117.5}$)	119			
	Petty cash (47 × $^{17.5}/_{117.5}$)	7			
	Balance c/f	47,344			
		48,084			48,084
			2/4/X5	Balance b/f	47,344

DEBTORS' LEDGER

Wells Stores

Date	Details	Amount £	Date	Details	Amount £
1/4/X5	Balance b/f	8,077	1/4/X5	Sales returns	112
	Sales day book	3,447		Cash received	5,237
				Discount allowed	105
				Balance b/f	6,070
		11,524			11,524
2/4/X5	Balance b/f	6,070			

Lawrence & Sons

Date	Details	Amount £	Date	Details	Amount £
1/4/X5	Balance b/f	6,598	1/4/X5	Cash received	3,069
	Sales day book	6,377		Discount allowed	62
				Balance c/f	9,844
		12,975			12,975
2/4/X5	Balance b/f	9,844			

Grenfell Bros

Date	Details	Amount £	Date	Details	Amount £
1/4/X5	Balance b/f	29,514	1/4/X5	Sales returns	284
	Sales day book	11,549		Cash received	4,794
				Discount allowed	96
				Balance b/f	35,889
		41,063			41,063
2/4/X5	Balance b/f	35,889			

	£	£
Updated debtors' control account balance		557,304

	£
Updated customer balances	
Garnett Ltd (9,423 + 4,413)	13,836
Wells Stores	6,070
Lawrence & Sons	9,844
Shields Ltd (8,614 + 2,791)	11,405
Nicolson Partnership (37,983 + 34,950 – 3,725)	69,208
Grenfell Bros	35,889
Malory Homecare Ltd	3,957
Nesbit Ltd (1,702 + 1,000 – 2,397 – 48)	257
Other customers (378,955 + 27,883)	406,838

	£
Total updated customer balances	557,304

List of updated balances at the end of the day on 1 April 19X5:

	Debit £	Credit £
Purchases [2,647,883 + (800 × $^{100}/_{117.5}$)]	2,648,564	
Sales		3,196,319
Sales returns (6,358 + 3,507)	9,865	
Telephones (734 – 31)	703	
Office expenses	9,611	
Interest (1,211 + 86)	1,297	
VAT		47,344
Debtors' control account	557,304	
Creditors' control account		307,332
Discounts allowed (15,898 + 311)	16,209	
Bank	16,068	
Petty cash	108	
Other debit balances	808,140	
Other credit balances		516,874
	4,067,869	4,067,869

SESSION 13

1   (a)   Yes
     (b)   No
     (c)   Yes
     (d)   No
     (e)   Yes

2

Code	Customer	Total £	Current £	30+ £	60+ £
F1	Farden's Garden Supplies	394.22	163.40	129.53	101.29

3   (a)   Debtors ledger clerk

     (b)   Debtors ledger clerk

     (c)   Someone independent of the debtors ledger clerk, such as the payroll clerk or financial accountant

     (d)   Sales manager

     (e)   Credit controller

4   When the customer receives the supplier's statement, its contents will be scrutinised and any discrepancies queried with the supplier. This may highlight errors in the recording of transactions in the debtors ledger and therefore act as an internal control.

5   (a)   Discounts are used to encourage customers to pay early and thus improve the cashflow of the business. An overdraft would be reduced cutting interest charges or bank balance and interest increased by early payment.

       (b)   A business will allow some leeway on a credit account as a gesture of goodwill. Rigid adherence to the 30-day time limit might mean valued customers are lost. (The customer may not have paid due to dissatisfaction with the goods or services provided.)

6

> Humphries Ltd
> 2 Hanover Street
> Bolton
> BL1 8ZA

> 15 March 19X3

Mr Bone
Bone's Phones
29 Park Square
Chorley
CH3 1PD

Dear Mr Bone

Queries on statement of account at 28 February 19X3

With reference to your letter of 8 March 19X3 I set out below an explanation for your queries.

(1)   Cheque not shown on statement

       Your cheque for £430 was not received by us until 1 March and consequently did not appear on the statement at 28 February. It will, however, appear on the statement issued on 31 March.

(2)   Disputed invoice H413

       We accept that the goods invoiced did not reach your premises and a credit note is to be issued with due haste. I apologise for the delay in resolving this matter.

       Please do not hesitate to contact me should you require any further information on these matters.

       Yours sincerely

       J Potter
       Credit controller

SESSION 14

1   This is a branch of civil law.

2   No, Freda is incorrect. The price of £39 is an invitation to treat and it is Freda who makes the offer to buy the dress for £39. The proprietor of the boutique then makes a counter-offer of £59.

3   William posted the letter of acceptance before the offer had expired and therefore would succeed if he sued Fred for breach of contract.

4   (a)   There is no contract between Mr and Mrs Wright as it is presumed that there is no intention to create legal relations in domestic arrangements.

     (b)   The arrangement with Mrs Scrubbitt is of a commercial nature, so the intention to create legal relations is presumed and therefore there will be a contract between the Wrights and Mrs Scrubbitt.

5   (a)   Yes
     (b)   Yes, in the form of a deed.
     (c)   No, although they usually are.

6   This means that both parties must do or promise to do something as their side of the contract. For example, Jim agrees to pay Adrian £50 cash to buy Adrian's Matterblaster guitar. The £50 and the guitar constitute each party's consideration.

SESSION 15

1   A purchase order will be raised.

2   A goods received note is completed by the goods-inwards officials, detailing all the goods in a delivery. This can then be matched with the supplier's own documentation, the despatch or delivery note, to ensure agreement with the supplier's records. This will highlight any shortfalls or incorrect deliveries at an early stage. The goods received note is also matched with the purchase invoice to ensure that the business does not pay for goods that have not been received. The goods received note is also matched with the purchase order and sales order from the supplier to ensure that the original order is what has been received.

3   The stamp will contain boxes to be completed giving details of the business' own sequential number, date of receipt, nominal ledger code for goods received, supplier code and a signature of authorisation.

4   For some services received, there will be an advice note or a contract which can be checked; otherwise, the department head's authorisation should only be given if he or she is satisfied with the service given.

5   VAT can be reclaimed only by a business registered for VAT. It must hold a VAT invoice from a supplier that is registered for VAT and the invoice must be for allowable expenditure.

6

Crackpotts
2 High Street
Sheffield
S1 8UV

4 May 19X4

Sales ledger clerk
5 Meadowhall Street
Sheffield
S16 2PT

Dear Sir

Overcharge on invoice 237

We received a delivery of 30 teapots from you on 22 April, as detailed on your delivery note 8834. However, your invoice 237 which we received on 3 May was for 35 teapots.

Please would you issue a credit note in respect of the overcharge of £60 plus VAT and send it to us as soon as possible.

I look forward to hearing from you.

Yours faithfully

A White
Creditor's ledger clerk

SESSION 16

1   (a)   Yes

    (b)   No, irrecoverable VAT would not be analysed out separately, but included under the appropriate purchases heading with the price of that item.

    (c)   No, discount received will be recovered when the invoice is paid.

    (d)   No, discount allowed relates to customers and is nothing to do with purchases and payments.

    (e)   No, the purchase day book only records credit purchases.

2

Date	Invoice No.	Code	Supplier	Total £	VAT £	01 £	02 £	03 £	04 £
1 Aug	84	C07	Cutefrocks	27.00		27.00			
3 Aug	85	B02	Bella Ltd	158.63	23.63		135.00		
4 Aug	86	M03	Mood Food Ltd	505.25					505.25

3

	£	£
Debit		
Raw materials – steel	2,439	
Raw materials – wood	751	
Components	203	
Sundries	76	
Subcontractors	600	
Electricity	185	
Fixed assets – car	14,000	
VAT control account	745	
Credit		
Creditor's ledger control account		18,999
	18,999	18,999

4 Yes, both these books list all purchase invoices received for credit transactions.

5 The purchase invoice register lists all invoices received prior to their dissemination to the various department heads who authorise them. Only authorised invoices are entered in the purchase day book and then marked off in the register as transferred.

A review of the purchase invoice register would highlight any invoices that were being queried or mislaid. This acts as an internal control preventing errors in the recording of purchases.

6 The allocation of a sequential number and review of the sequence ensures the completeness of recording of purchase invoices. This would not be possible if the suppliers' numbers were relied upon as they bear no relation to one another; invoices from a particular supplier will not form a complete sequence and different suppliers have different sequences of invoice numbers.

SESSION 17

1 (a) Nominal (or general) ledger
    (b) Creditors ledger
    (c) Debtors ledger
    (d) Nominal ledger

2 Discount received is a debit entry in a creditor's individual account.

3

	£
2 boxes of envelopes (2 × £7.50)	15.00
VAT (15 × 17.5%	2.63
	17.63

£17.63 will be recorded in Karen Kreb's creditors ledger account.

4   (a)   Liability
   (b)   Income
   (c)   Expense
   (d)   Asset

5

	£
Original total	4,966
(a) Debit balance listed as credit balance	(860)
(b) Balance omitted	620
	4,726

The corrected total of the list of balances is £4,726.

6

A Bay & Co
42 Town Chambers
Basildon
BA2 8FR

18 February 19X8

Mr C Harley
Harley Co Ltd
7 Wensbury Way
Basildon
BA5 2JA

Dear Mr Harley

Creditors ledger reconciliation

Thank you for your recent inquiry regarding controls over payments to suppliers and I detail below how reconciliation is performed.

(1)   All the accounts in the creditor's ledger are balanced at the end of each month and a list of these balances compiled and totalled.

(2)   A balance is also struck on the creditor's ledger control account at the end of each month.

(3)   The totals of the list of balances and the control account are compared. All discrepancies should be investigated and adjusted for.

(4) As John Conn is to perform this reconciliation I suggest that you review it and authorise the adjustments before they are made.

This control will help to ensure that recording of transactions with creditors is accurate.

Please do not hesitate to contact me should you require any further information.

Yours sincerely

J Bay
A Bay & Co

Bookkeeping exercise

DEBTORS' LEDGER

Willowes Ltd

Date	Details	Amount £	Date	Details	Amount £
1/5/X5	Balance b/f	442	1/5/X5	Cash receipts	435
	Credit sales	627	31/5/X5	Balance c/f	634
		1,069			1,069
1/6/X5	Balance b/f	634			

Howard & Howard

Date	Details	Amount £	Date	Details	Amount £
1/5/X5	Balance b/f	387	1/5/X5	Cash receipts	371
	Credit sales	360	31/5/X5	Balance c/f	376
		747			747
1/6/X5	Balance b/f	376			

Chapman Ltd

Date	Details	Amount £	Date	Details	Amount £
1/5/X5	Credit sales	729	1/5/X5	Balance b/f	83
				Cash receipts	452
				Discounts allowed	16
			31/5/X5	Balance c/f	178
		729			729
1/6/X5	Balance b/f	178			

Beaumann & Baker

Date	Details	Amount £	Date	Details	Amount £
1/5/X5	Balance b/f	320	1/5/X5	Cash receipts	251
			31/5/X5	Balance c/f	69
		320			320
1/6/X5	Balance b/f	69			

Other customers

Date	Details	Amount £	Date	Details	Amount £
1/5/X5	Balance b/f	35,474	1/5/X5	Cash receipts	34,633
	Credit sales	43,394		Discounts allowed	102
			31/5/X5	Balance c/f	44,133
		78,868			78,868
	Balance b/f	44,133			

CREDITORS' LEDGER

Atwood & Co

Date	Details	Amount £	Date	Details	Amount £
1/5/X5	Cash payments	4,069	1/5/X5	Balance b/f	4,069
31/5/X5	Balance c/f	5,730		Credit purchases	5,730
		9,799			9,799
				Balance b/f	5,730

Karlin & Partners

Date	Details	Amount £	Date	Details	Amount £
1/5/X5	Cash payments	3,415	1/5/X5	Balance b/f	3,503
	Discount received	87		Credit purchases	4,455
31/5/X5	Balance c/f	4,456			
		7,958			7,958
			1/6/X5	Balance b/f	4,456

Hardy Ltd

Date	Details	Amount £	Date	Details	Amount £
1/5/X5	Cash payments	2,418	1/5/X5	Balance b/f	2,794
31/5/X5	Balance c/f	2,458		Credit purchases	2,082
		4,876			4,876
			1/6/X5	Balance b/f	2,458

Other suppliers

Date	Details	Amount £	Date	Details	Amount £
1/5/X5	Cash payments	14,237	1/5/X5	Balance b/f	9,705
	Discount received	134		Credit purchases	14,788
31/5/X5	Balance c/f	10,122			
		24,493			24,493
			1/6/X5	Balance b/f	10,122

GENERAL LEDGER

Sales

Date	Details	Amount £	Date	Details	Amount £
			1/5/X5	Balance b/f	91,615
				Credit sales	38,391
			31/5/X5	Balance b/f	130,006

Purchases

Date	Details	Amount £	Date	Details	Amount £
1/5/X5	Balance b/f	56,776			
	Credit purchases	18,976			
31/5/X5	Balance b/f	75,752			

Debtors' control account

Date	Details	Amount £	Date	Details	Amount £
1/5/X5	Balance b/f	36,623	1/5/X5	Balance b/f	83
	Credit sales	45,110		Cash received	36,142
				Discounts allowed	118
			31/5/X5	Balance c/f	45,390
		81,733			81,733
1/6/X5	Balance b/f	45,390			

Creditors' control account

Date	Details	Amount £	Date	Details	Amount £
1/5/X5	Cash payments	24,139	1/5/X5	Balance b/f	20,071
	Discounts received	221		Credit purchases	27,055
31/5/X5	Balance c/f	22,766			
		47,126			47,126
			1/6/X5	Balance b/f	22,766

VAT account

Date	Details	Amount £	Date	Details	Amount £
1/5/X5	Credit purchases	4,021	1/5/X5	Balance b/f	16,195
	Cash payments	8,061		Credit sales	6,719
	Petty cash	5			
31/5/X5	Balance c/f	10,827			
		22,914			22,914
			1/6/X5	Balance b/f	10,827

Discounts allowed

Date	Details	Amount £	Date	Details	Amount £
1/5/X5	Balance b/f	297			
	Discounts allowed	118			
31/5/X5	Balance b/f	415			

Discounts received

Date	Details	Amount £	Date	Details	Amount £
			1/5/X5	Balance b/f	564
				Discounts received	221
			31/5/X5	Balance b/f	785

Stock

Date	Details	Amount £	Date	Details	Amount £
1/5/X5	Balance b/f	37,415			

Wages and salaries

Date	Details	Amount £	Date	Details	Amount £
1/5/X5	Balance b/f	20,814			
	Cash payments	9,151			
31/5/X5	Balance b/f	29,965			

Postage and stationery

Date	Details	Amount £	Date	Details	Amount £
1/5/X5	Balance b/f	1,247			
	Credit purchases	476			
	Petty cash	11			
		1,734			
31/5/X5	Balance b/f	1,734			

Travel and subsistence

Date	Details	Amount £	Date	Details	Amount £
1/5/X5	Balance b/f	757			
	Credit purchases	306			
	Petty cash	17			
		1,080			
31/5/X5	Balance b/f	1,080			

Other expenditure

Date	Details	Amount £	Date	Details	Amount £
1/5/X5	Balance b/f	3,432			
	Credit purchases	1,800			
	Petty cash	14			
		5,246			
31/5/X5	Balance b/f	5,246			

Telephones

Date	Details	Amount £	Date	Details	Amount £
1/5/X5	Credit purchases	566			

Repairs and renewals

Date	Details	Amount £	Date	Details	Amount £
1/5/X5	Balance b/f	697			
	Credit purchases	910			
		1,607			
31/5/X5	Balance b/f	1,607			

Fixed assets

Date	Details	Amount £	Date	Details	Amount £
1/5/X5	Balance b/f	171,450			

Capital

Date	Details	Amount £	Date	Details	Amount £
			1/5/X5	Balance b/f	233,643

General ledger balances at 31 May 19X5

	Debit £	Credit £
Sales		130,006
Purchases	75,752	
Debtors' control account	45,390	
Creditors' control account		22,766
VAT		10,827
Discounts allowed	415	
Discounts received		785
Stock	37,415	
Wages and salaries	29,965	
Postage and stationery	1,734	
Travel and subsistence	1,080	
Other expenditure	5,246	
Telephones	566	
Repairs and renewals	1,607	
Fixed assets	171,450	
Capital and reserves		233,643
Cash at bank	27,394	
Petty cash	13	
Total	398,027	398,027

SESSION 18

1   The price invoiced of 40p per litre will be the price on the credit note.

2   A returns outwards note is used to record returns to suppliers.

A four-part set would be used as follows:

• Part one is sent to the supplier with the goods.

• Part two is kept in despatch.

• Part three is sent to the stores department to update their record.

• Part four is sent to the creditors' ledger department for checking with the credit note.

3   The incorrect invoice should be processed as usual, the credit note will cancel it when processed.

4   (a)   Debit   Janitorial Supplies Ltd   £117.50

			£	£
(b)	Debit	Creditors' ledger control account	117.50	
	Credit	Purchases		100.00
		VAT control account		17.50

5

Creditors' ledger control account

	£		£
Cash	11,400	Balance b/f	1,890
Discounts received	840		
Credit notes	756	Purchase invoices	12,000
Balance c/f	894		
	———		———
	13,890		13,890
	———		———

The balance on the creditors ledger control account on 30 September 19X1 is £894.

6 (a) Yes, as the total will be posted to the control account.
(b) No
(c) No

Bookkeeping exercise

GENERAL LEDGER

Debtors' control account

Date	Details	Amount £	Date	Details	Amount £
1/3/X4	Balance b/f	497,061	1/3/X4	Cash received	4,331
	Sales day book	25,968		Discount allowed	87
				Balance c/f	518,611
		———			———
		523,029			523,029
		———			———
2/3/X4	Balance b/f	518,611			

Creditors' control account

Date	Details	Amount £	Date	Details	Amount £
1/3/X4	Purchases returns	3,208	1/3/X4	Balance b/f	305,825
	Cash paid	17,575		Purchases day book	38,043
	Discount received	118			
	Balance c/f	322,967			
		———			———
		343,967			343,868
		———			———
			2/3/X4	Balance b/f	322,967

Telephone

Date	Details	Amount £	Date	Details	Amount £
1/3/X4	Balance b/f	–	1/3/X4	Balance c/f	716
	Purchases day book	716			
		716			716
2/3/X4	Balance b/f	716			

Purchases

Date	Details	Amount £	Date	Details	Amount £
1/3/X4	Balance b/f	2,543,560	1/3/X4	Balance c/f	2,575,769
	Purchases day book	31,662			
	Cash paid (643 – 96)	547			
		2,575,769			2,575,769
2/3/X4	Balance b/f	2,575,769			

VAT

Date	Details	Amount £	Date	Details	Amount £
1/3/X4	Purchase day book	5,665	1/3/X4	Balance b/f	72,108
	Cash purchases	96		Sales day book	3,868
	Balance c/f	70,693		Purchases returns	478
		76,454			76,454
			2/3/X4	Balance b/f	70,693

CREDITORS' LEDGER

Prittchett Ltd

Date	Details	Amount £	Date	Details	Amount £
1/3/X4	Paid paid	640	1/3/X4	Balance b/f	23,820
	Balance c/f	34,810		Purchases day book	11,630
		35,450			35,450
			2/3/X4	Balance b/f	34,810

Murdoch Bros

Date	Details	Amount £	Date	Details	Amount £
1/3/X4	Purchases returns	2,115	1/3/X4	Balance b/f	8,123
	Cash paid	5,890		Purchases day book	8,863
	Discount received	118			
	Balance c/f	8,863			
		16,986			16,986
			2/3/X4	Balance b/f	8,863

Selincourt & Partners

Date	Details	Amount £	Date	Details	Amount £
1/3/X4	Purchases returns	1,093	1/3/X4	Balance b/f	6,543
	Cash paid	1,529		Purchases day book	3,782
	Balance c/f	7,703			
		10,325			10,325
			2/3/X4	Balance b/f	7,703

List of updated balances at the end of the day:

	Debit balances £	Credit balances £
Suppliers		
Prittchett Ltd		34,810
Murdoch Bros		8,863
Selincourt & Partners		7,703
English Telecomm		841
Other suppliers (267,339 + 12,927 – 9,516)		270,750
Total		322,967
Creditors' control account		322,967

	Debit balances £	Credit balances £
Purchases	2,575,769	
Sales (4,173,893 + 22,100)		4,195,993
Sales returns	11,084	
Purchases returns (10,926 + 2,730)		13,656
Debtors' control account	518,611	
Creditors' control account		322,967
Telephone	716	
Rent payable (5,000 + 2,500)	7,500	
Bank charges (91 + 45)	136	
VAT		70,693
Bank (15,398 + 4,331 – 20,763)		1,034
Discount allowed (20,319 + 87)	20,406	
Discount received (9,627 + 118)		9,745
Other debit balances	2,002,119	
Other credit balances		522,253
	———	———
Total	5,136,341	5,136,341

SESSION 19

1   (a) and (b) will be deducted from the balance per suppliers' statement.

2   The creditors' ledger requires amendment by debiting IC Frozen Foods Ltd's account with £594. The nominal ledger needs adjusting by debiting the creditors' ledger control account by £594 and crediting the purchase account by £594.

3   No amendments are required to the ledgers as the discrepancies are entirely in respect of items in transit:

	£
Balance per supplier's statement	3,286.20
Less: Cash in transit	(873.18)
Less: Goods in transit	(126.20)
	———
Balance per creditors' ledger account	2,286.82

4   Invoices and suppliers' statements often have a detachable remittance advice.

5   (a)   No
     (b)   Yes
     (c)   No

6

Astro Models Ltd
12 Vicarge Lane
Tenbury Wells
Shropshire
BN4 8AL

Debtors Ledger Clerk
Aeropics Ltd
Unit 4
Townview Estate
West Bromwich
B17 6LV

10 July

Dear Sir

Settlement discounts allowed

I refer to your invoices 00851 and 00863 for which payment was made, in accordance with your terms of trade, after deduction of a 2% settlement discount. I note from the supplier's statement for June that you have not deducted this discount from our account, although the payments do appear and are within the time limit stipulated.

I would be grateful if you could amend our account to reflect the discount taken as soon as possible.

Yours faithfully

J Parker
Creditors ledger clerk